ITALIA! ITALIA!

ITALIA!

VALENTINA HARRIS

ITALIA!

A Passion for the Real Food of Italy

PHOTOGRAPHS BY MARTIN BRIGDALE

CASSELL

Acknowledgements and Dedication

I would like to thank the tireless Wendy Hobson for once again helping me to marshal this book into order. Thank you also to Deborah Taylor for letting me persuade her that I should write it, and good luck in your new career.

This book is dedicated to all the people who have ever attended any of my courses; you were the ones who made it all really happen. But most of all this book is for Judith Sweet, who lived through most of the best and the worst bits with me, and who is so precious to me both in and out of any kitchen.

This edition first published in the UK 1999 by
Cassell
Wellington House
125 Strand
London WC2R 0BB
www.cassell.co.uk

Text copyright © Valentina Harris 1999

Food photography © Martin Brigdale 1999

British Library Cataloguing-in-Publication Data
A catalogue record for this book is available from the British Library

ISBN 0-304-35150-4

Edited by Wendy Hobson
Designed and typeset by Harry Green
Home economist Maxine Clark
Food styling by Helen Trent
Printed and bound by
South China Printing Co. Ltd, Hong Kong

Notes on the Recipes

Spoon measurements are level.

1 tablespoon is 15 ml;
1 teaspoon is 5 ml.

Eggs are large.

Wash, trim and peel fresh produce, as appropriate, before preparation.

A wine glass is about 150 ml (5 fl oz).

Follow one set of measurements only; do not mix metric and imperial.

Adjust seasoning or strongly flavoured ingredients to taste.

The portions specified tend to be fairly generous.

Contents

Introduction

Cooks in search of the real Italy . . .

I have been wanting to write this book ever since I first began to teach cookery courses in Italy. I began the courses not because I thought they would ever be particularly lucrative, but because my enormous passion and heartfelt love for Italy, her food and her culture, is something which I have spent all my professional life trying to share. What better way could there be of expressing this passion than by actually taking people by the hand and showing them what all my books, TV programmes, magazine articles, and cookery demonstrations – carried out literally all over the world – have been conveying for so many years?

It is through the events which occurred on these courses that this book was born. It is the collection of the best recipes taught there, experiments in the kitchen, evolution of old recipes, and revival of traditional recipes which had been almost abandoned in the face of microwaves.

However, *Italia! Italia!* is much more than that. Linking the book together is a collection of stories about the people on those courses, the experiences we had together either in the kitchen, round the table or on days out. For me, these tales are in turn moving, funny, endearing, happy, sad or just plain hilarious. All the cooks featured in this book were there because of their love of Italian food and wine, and their love of Italy. In practically every course, human relationships flourished, friendships were made and long-lasting bonds were forged.

If you thought this book was going to be another collection of recipes from Italy, think again. The recipes are there – and they are tried and tested by many more people than the average cookery book – but I hope that in reading about what we got up to whilst cooking, you can absorb a little of the experience of actually being there – and wish that you had been!

As the courses I have taught have taken place in Piemonte, Toscana, Veneto and Sicilia, there is a cross-section of recipes from all these regions, always respecting the best of local tradition and the seasonal availability of ingredients.

1 Antipasti

In a traditional Italian meal, the antipasto is the very first part of what is going to be a long, special meal – in fact, it means 'before the meal', so the meal itself doesn't really begin until the next course.

Everyday meals in Italy tend to be shorter and with fewer courses, so often the antipasto either replaces another course or it becomes the whole meal, perhaps with a bowl of salad as a partner. It is always a very light course, can be hot or cold, and made using seafood, meat, vegetables, cheese or fruit, or a whole range of combinations.

Eating antipasto is a time-honoured ritual going back to the days of Ancient Rome, where these sorts of dish formed part of interminable dinners at sundown, and subsequently, as leftovers, were served for breakfast next morning. These days, if one is going to have a long, traditional meal with lots of courses, it often happens at lunchtime, and the evening meal which follows tends to be light and lean: perhaps a bowl of soup and a little bread and fruit.

An antipasto can be as simple as a small dish of olives and a few breadsticks, or even just bread, and as complicated as a dish of marinated fish fillets in a light sauce. It is the part of the meal where Italy's plethora of cured meats really come into their own, with classics like prosciutto crudo with melon or figs, paper-thin bresaola sprinkled with finely chopped red onion, or a selection of different kinds of salami.

Having enjoyed the antipasto, the meal really begins with a course of either pasta, risotto, soup, gnocchi or another similar first-course dish. This is then followed by the main meat or fish course with vegetables. Cheese, if it is going to be served at all, is served next, and finally dessert, fruit, coffee and after-dinner drinks. And then, of course, a long siesta . . .

Whipped Salt Cod in the Venetian Style
Baccalà Mantecato alla Veneziana

This is not an easy dish to make but it is so very delicious that I felt it had to be included. If you have ever eaten it at any of the many bars of Venice, you may be wondering how it is made, so even if you don't make it more than once, you will at least know how they achieve that fantastically smooth, light, fluffy texture. Should you be having difficulty in getting the fish going once you have boned and skinned it, you can beat it first in a pestle and mortar, or put it in a bowl over a pan of simmering water and mash it with a fork to soften it enough to help you work with it. *Baccalà* is dried salt cod, which needs several days of soaking in fresh, cold water to reconstitute it. *Stoccafisso* is dried salt herring, which is treated in the same way and has a stronger flavour than *baccalà*.

SERVES 6

1 kg (3 lb) *baccalà* or *stoccafisso*

up to 350 ml (12 fl oz) extra virgin olive oil

4 tablespoons finely chopped fresh
   flatleaf parsley

2–4 garlic cloves, crushed

salt and freshly milled black pepper

TO SERVE

toasted ciabatta or other coarse
   Italian bread

Soak the salt fish for at least two days in fresh, cold water, changing the water two or three times each day.

Rinse the soaked fish carefully, then blanch in boiling water for 1 minute. Drain thoroughly, then pat dry and cool until cold enough to handle. The fish must be quite dry before you start. Remove all the skin and every single bone.

Transfer to a deep bowl and reduce to flakes, then begin to 'whip' the fish with a large wooden spoon, gradually adding the olive oil in a fine stream, as though you were making mayonnaise. The quantity of oil will depend on the greasiness of the fish and how good the oil is. Stop whipping when the fish has become rather like whipped cream: white and light and fluffy. Stir in chopped parsley, garlic salt and pepper to taste (be very careful not to oversalt) and chill until ready to serve as a dip or on toasted ciabatta bread.

Grilled Mixed Seafood
Frutti di Mare Gratinati

A lovely, simple antipasto which makes the most of the deliciously fresh selection of seafood available from the fish markets of Venice. As with any seafood dish, it is the freshness of the raw material which makes all the difference. It is far better to reduce the number of choices to one or two and have them really fresh, rather than trying to serve lots of different varieties that may not be in their prime.

SERVES 4

16 fresh, live mussels
  in their shells

8 oysters

4 fresh razor shells

20 large clams

4 scallops

4 tablespoons fresh breadcrumbs

4 tablespoons freshly grated
  Parmesan cheese

3 garlic cloves, finely chopped

3 tablespoons chopped fresh parsley

salt and freshly milled black pepper

5 tablespoons olive oil

Carefully clean and scrub all the shellfish well, scraping off any barnacles and removing the little beard at the side of the mussels. Soak for 30 minutes or so each time in two or three changes of fresh, clean water, rinsing thoroughly between each soak. Discard any open ones which do not close when tapped sharply. Drain well. Place in a large pan, cover and steam over a high heat for 5–8 minutes, just until they open up. Take them off the heat and out of the pan to cool so that they don't overcook. Discard *all* those which have not opened. Reserve the juices in the pan for another dish.

Place all the shellfish on the half shell and put them all into a wide, flameproof dish or on a baking sheet. Mix together all the remaining ingredients except the olive oil, then spoon over the top of each shellfish. Drizzle with the olive oil, being generous with the oil as this recipe must not turn out dry. Place the dish or baking sheet under a hot grill for 5 minutes to brown, then serve at once on individual plates.

Cold Veal with Tuna Mayonnaise
Vitello Tonnato

This is the very first thing I ever made for my husband to eat and he thought it was really horrible! It was a great shame because I think it is delicious – but perhaps it just didn't turn out so well that day . . . ? To make the mayonnaise easily, put one egg into the bowl of the food processor and whizz with the blade until pale yellow, then gradually add 150 ml (5 fl oz) each of sunflower oil and extra virgin olive oil, mixed together, in a very thin, slow, steady stream, keeping the motor running. Gradually, the oil and egg will emulsify and turn into a thick, smooth, pale texture. Add the juice of half a lemon and season to taste.

SERVES 6

900 g (2 lb) veal fillet joint

600 ml (1 pint) veal or chicken stock

FOR THE MARINADE

1 bottle of dry white wine

1 onion, sliced

1 carrot, sliced

4 cloves

3 bay leaves, chopped

salt and freshly milled black pepper

FOR THE SAUCE

300 g (11 oz) thick mayonnaise (see above)

150 g (5 oz) canned tuna fish in olive oil, drained
   and finely flaked

salt and freshly milled black pepper

2 handfuls of salted capers, rinsed and finely chopped

the reserved glass of wine (see method)

TO GARNISH

black olives, capers, gherkins, slices of lemon and
   chopped fresh parsley

Lay the veal joint in a deep bowl. Reserve one glass of the wine for the sauce, then mix the rest of the wine with the remaining marinade ingredients and pour over the meat. Cover and leave to stand overnight.

Next day, drain the meat from the marinade, wrap it and tie it up in a muslin cloth, then lay it in a deep pan. Pour the marinade and the stock over the meat, bring to the boil, cover and simmer gently for about 1½ hours or until the meat is completely cooked through. Leave the meat to cool in the marinade.

Remove the meat from the cold marinade and unwrap it. Slice it thinly on to a large, flat platter. Mix the mayonnaise with the other sauce ingredients, then coat the sliced meat completely with the sauce. Garnish the platter and serve at once, or chill until required. Don't serve too cold.

Yellow Peppers with Anchovy Sauce
Antipasto di Peperoni

I always prefer to use salted anchovies instead of the more readily available anchovies in olive oil as they have a much stronger, fuller flavour. If you use canned anchovies, you'll need to use double the amount and they will already be filleted for you. The main thing is to remember about salted anchovies is that they do need rinsing very thoroughly.

SERVES 4–6

100 g (4 oz) salted anchovies, boned and rinsed

2 garlic cloves, chopped

50 ml (2 fl oz) olive oil

25 g (I oz) unsalted butter

7 tablespoons milk

4 sweet, juicy yellow peppers, seeded and cut into strips

Fry the anchovies gently with the garlic, olive oil and butter, mixing to make a smooth brown purée. Dilute with the milk, then stir in the peppers. Cook gently for about 30 minutes, spooning the anchovy sauce over the peppers as they cook, until the peppers are completely floppy and soft. Serve hot as an antipasto.

Hot Anchovy Dip for Vegetables
Bagna Cauda

The easiest way to serve the *bagna cauda* is to pour it into a fondue set and keep the heat low so that it stays warm but does not cook any further. All the vegetables listed below are traditionally used for the dish but you can choose which ones you want to use and leave others out, or simply choose your own. Those vegetables which are cooked, such as potatoes, are usually served very hot as a contrast to the cold, raw vegetables.

SERVES 4

Jerusalem artichokes, peeled

cauliflower florets

red and green peppers, seeded
   and cut into strips

crisp white cabbage leaves

turnips, peeled, boiled and cut into strips

potatoes, peeled, boiled and
   cut into strips

carrots, cut into strips

button onions, lightly boiled

fennel bulbs, quartered

globe artichokes, prepared
   and served raw or cooked

FOR THE DIP

150 ml (5 fl oz) olive oil

3 garlic cloves, thinly sliced

1½ salted anchovies, boned and rinsed

1 heaped tablespoon unsalted butter

a pinch of salt

½ tomato, peeled and chopped (optional)

3 tablespoons single cream (optional)

Prepare the vegetables and arrange them on a platter in an attractive pattern.

Heat the olive oil until sizzling hot, then add the garlic and fry until golden. Add the anchovies, lower the heat and cook gently until the anchovies have all dissolved into the oil, stirring regularly. Stir in the butter and add a little salt to taste. If you wish, add the chopped tomato and cream, stir and heat through briefly. Serve the dip very hot.

Fried Crispy Dough Squares
Crescentine Salate

When I was a child, this is the sort of thing which would be made for us for afternoon snack time: *merenda*. The smell of the frying dough would drift through the kitchen window and draw us from our various activities to wait under the sill. Nowadays, they are a nostalgic part of my repertoire and I serve them piping hot with drinks before lunch or dinner.

SERVES 4

250 g (9 oz) plain white flour

1 teaspoon dried yeast

a pinch of salt

25 g (1 oz) lard or unsalted butter, diced

120 ml (4 fl oz) warm beef stock

flour for dusting

olive or sunflower oil for deep-frying

(or half oil and half lard)

Tip the flour on to the work top and make a hollow in the centre. Add the yeast, salt and lard or butter and knead together, adding the stock a little at a time and using just enough to blend the ingredients together. Make a dough which is slightly softer than pasta dough but not as soft as bread dough; the texture of shortcrust pastry is about right. Roll out the dough to a 25 cm (10 in) square on a lightly floured surface. Fold it in half, then in half again. Roll it out to the original size again, then fold it into four as before. Repeat this process several times, then roll it out to about 2 mm thick. Cut it into rectangular shapes about the size of a matchbox.

Heat the oil or oil and lard until a small piece of bread dropped into it sizzles instantly. Fry the crisps in the oil in batches until golden, crisp and puffed. They will cook in 1–2 minutes so watch them carefully. Scoop them out of the oil, drain on kitchen paper and sprinkle with salt. Serve piping hot.

Buying Knives in Lucca

One of the things which many of my students want to do when they come on a course is to equip their kitchen with traditional Italian implements, so a morning or an afternoon is always dedicated to a spree in the local kitchen equipment shops. The items most usually carried away to the four corners of the globe are things like *frittata* pans, pasta colanders, polenta sieves, mezzaluna choppers and olive oil pourers. It seems that only in Italy can one find a *frittata* pan that will really let the *frittata* turn over, a colander that will safely and accurately drain away all the water from the pasta, a sieve which will make polenta feel like talcum powder, a mezzaluna that will make the art of chopping herbs incredibly easy, and a little lidded jug with a spout so narrow it will allow you to pour out the oil in a fine, golden-green stream. Or are they just buying these things because they look so attractive and because I am there to point out the benefits?

In any case, whatever the reason for buying, everyone always seems to go back laden with all sorts of items from the local *casalinghi* and I am only hopeful that they are put to good use once they are in their own kitchens. I should hate to think that those hours spent choosing and trying things out might end up with a lovingly bought bag of utensils lying forgotten in a drawer.

Those who are most keen are easily distinguishable by the fact that they want to buy knives. In Lucca, there is a knife shop in a tiny, medieval back street which is no bigger than the average spare bedroom, yet it exudes so much olde worlde charm as to be a must for any serious kitchen-knife expert or even not-so-expert. The old man who owns the shop asks first to see your hands, which he stares at intently before holding your wrist and examining your fingers and palm minutely. Then he begins to open some of the several hundred small drawers which line the shop and brings out knives of varying shapes, sizes and weights, of many different brands and prices. Needless to say, he is alone in the popular shop and a queue is now forming half way down the street. You may be there only to buy an inexpensive vegetable knife, but he always treats you as though you are the most important, and the only, customer he will be dealing with that day.

You can imagine the time it took to equip ten people with about six knives each! A large cook's knife, a small cook's knife, a boning knife, a fish knife, a vegetable knife

and a paring knife are always a good basis for any serious cook, and of course the knife has to feel right as well as looking the part, plus it must be easy to sharpen well, for nothing is more frustrating than a blunt edge. I always warn my eager students to learn the art of sharpening the knife they are buying at the time of purchase, so they will not be bitterly disappointed later on. Though your knife-buying experience might not have the care and expertise of the 'Lucca knife man', as he is known fondly by all those who have stepped into his dingy, dark, fusty shop, most reputable dealers will know enough about the knives they are selling to tell you how to keep them razor sharp.

In Lucca, as in all Italian towns, you can have all your knives sharpened at a very reasonable price by the *arrotino*, or knife grinder. This is another poky shop that feels as though it has been here since the twelfth century and it too sells knives, although it is used principally for the owner's expertise in the ancient art of knife grinding. Overnight, your knives will be ready for collection with a fine, new bevelled edge, a sparkling, shiny surface and a blade that can cut clean, true and straight without too much pressure.

These shops, and many like them all over Italy, are to be preserved and even worshipped by anybody who, like my students and me, appreciate the inimitable craftsmanship of a proper knife, which is a joy to see and to use. I wish there were more shops like them everywhere, and I hope that those which do exist will not be swallowed up in the increasing tide of so-called progress and development.

Tuscan Bread and Tomato Salad
Panzanella

When I lived by the sea, I used to do a lot of boating. This salad was one of the great highlights of the day. We'd trail the stale loaf of bread behind the boat on the end of a rope until it was squashy, then we'd wrap it in a cloth and squeeze it dry. The bread would then be heaped on to the deck of the boat and we would slice the vegetables over the bread. Then we'd add a little olive oil, vinegar and pepper and we'd mix it all together with our bare hands. With our feet dangling in the perfectly clean, blue water, and no plates or cutlery, no salad has ever tasted so good.

SERVES 4

8 slices of stale coarse white Italian
    bread, such as ciabatta, pugliese
4 fist-sized ripe, fresh tomatoes,
    sliced or diced
1 large onion, sliced

1 large cucumber, sliced or diced
a handful of basil leaves,
    torn into small pieces
extra virgin olive oil
red wine vinegar
salt and freshly milled black pepper

Soak the bread in cold water for about 15 minutes. Squeeze the bread dry in a cloth. Mix the damp bread with the tomatoes, onion, cucumber and basil. Dress with olive oil, wine vinegar and salt and pepper to taste. Mix the ingredients together very thoroughly and leave to stand for about 1 hour before serving.

Tuscan Liver Pâté
Crostini

Some say that this is the original, fifteenth-century recipe for pâté, which was then exported to France along with various other recipes such as onion soup. It is a really wonderful dish, and in Tuscany the word *crostini* traditionally refers to this pâté, as opposed to toasted bread with various toppings.

SERVES 4

½ onion, finely chopped

1 carrot, finely chopped

1 celery stick, finely chopped

1 tablespoon finely chopped
  fresh parsley

3 tablespoons olive oil

40 g (1½ oz) unsalted butter

1 chicken liver, trimmed, washed and dried

100 g (4 oz) calves' liver, trimmed, washed and dried

2 tablespoons dry white wine

1 heaped tablespoon tomato purée

6 tablespoons hot water or stock

salt and freshly milled black pepper

25 g (1 oz) salted capers, rinsed and finely chopped

4–8 thin slices of crusty white or brown bread

Fry the vegetables and parsley in the olive oil and half of the butter until soft. Stir in the livers, add the wine and evaporate the wine for about 2 minutes. Mix the tomato purée with 4 tablespoons of the water or stock, then stir it into the pan with the remaining water and season to taste with salt and pepper. Cover and simmer for about 20 minutes.

Remove from the heat, lift the livers out of the sauce and mince or process them until smooth. Return the purée to the pan, stir in the remaining butter and all the capers and heat through gently. Remove from the heat and keep warm. Spread the bread generously with the liver topping and serve at once.

Marinated Green Olives
Olive Cunsati

This is a traditional Sicilian way of flavouring olives but you can try anything that takes your fancy. How about black olives just coated with olive oil, mixed with lots of freshly chopped rosemary leaves and a few slices of lemon? Add a handful of marinated olives to a dish of cured meats for a traditional antipasto.

SERVES 4

400 g (14 oz) green olives, stoned and crushed enough to crack them

50 g (2 oz) fresh dill, chopped

4 garlic cloves, crushed

15 fresh mint leaves

a pinch of salt

100 g (4 oz) small inner celery sticks with leaves, chopped

6 tablespoons extra virgin olive oil

8 tablespoons red wine vinegar

½ red chilli pepper, seeded and finely chopped

Put the olives into a bowl and add the dill, garlic, mint and salt. Cover with water and leave to soak for three days. Drain the olives well, then add the celery, olive oil and wine vinegar, then the chilli. Stir together thoroughly and serve.

Olive Pâté
Pate di Olive

You can smear this pâté on to thin slices of good-quality Italian bread, then add a slice of fresh, ripe tomato on top for a very simple but tasty antipasto. Alternatively, this pâté is served as a dip with bread or breadsticks.

SERVES 8

200 g (7 oz) black or green olives, stoned

grated zest and juice of ½ lemon

1 tablespoon extra virgin olive oil

50 g (2 oz) unsalted butter

15 g (½ oz) fresh white breadcrumbs

salt and freshly milled black pepper

Push the olives though a food mill or process in a food processor. Add the lemon zest and juice, olive oil, butter and breadcrumbs and process or mix together very thoroughly. Season with plenty of pepper and salt to taste. You should end up with a creamy, soft, smooth texture. Chill until required.

Chick Pea Flour Fritters
Panelle

As you wander about the markets of Palermo and other Sicilian towns, you'll find shops offering you *panelle* and other little snacks of this type to nibble as you walk around the streets.

SERVES 8

1 cup chick pea flour

6 cups water

2 tablespoons finely chopped fresh parsley

salt and freshly milled black pepper

vegetable oil for deep-frying

Put the chick pea flour in a pan and gradually add the water, stirring or whisking carefully to avoid the formation of lumps. Add the parsley, and salt and pepper to taste, and cook over a medium heat, stirring constantly, for about 45 minutes or until the mixture is very thick and just begins to stand away from the sides of the pan as you stir.

Working rapidly, pour the mixture on to a lightly oiled marble or wooden surface and spread it out with an oiled spatula into a thin sheet less than a 5 mm (¼ in) thick. When cooled, cut into about forty 5 x 7.5 cm (2 x 3 in) rectangles.

Heat a pan of vegetable oil deep enough to float the slices and fry them a few at a time for a few minutes, turning once, until both sides are pale golden brown. Drain on kitchen paper and serve hot.

Marinated Sardines
Sarde Marinate

It is really very important that the fish used for this recipe is absolutely fresh. In the absence of fresh fish, you could use smoked mackerel fillets instead, which will only need one day to marinate and can then be served immediately. Serve with a small tomato salad and some crusty bread.

SERVES 6

I kg (2¼ lb) freshest possible sardines
   or anchovies

150 ml (5 fl oz) white wine vinegar

2 garlic cloves, finely chopped

a handful of chopped fresh parsley

100 ml (3½ fl oz) olive oil

salt and freshly milled black pepper

Clean and wash the fish, carefully remove the bones and heads, then wash again and dry thoroughly. Lay the fish in a bowl. Mix together the wine vinegar, garlic and parsley and cover the fish with this mixture. Leave to stand in a cool place for about three days.

Rinse and dry the fish, then place it in a dry bowl. Mix the olive oil with a little salt and pepper, then pour it over the fish. Leave to marinate for two days in the fridge before serving.

Antipasto of Oranges
Antipasto d'Arance

Very unusual but nonetheless delicious, this dish is typical of southern Italy. It looks most impressive if you use a combination of blood oranges with ordinary oranges. You can garnish it with sprigs of flatleaf parsley if you wish.

SERVES 6

5 large oranges

150 g (5 oz) canned anchovy fillets, drained

½ wine glass of olive oil

salt

Wash the oranges carefully and slice them very thinly with their skins into neat rounds. Arrange the slices on a serving platter, place the anchovy fillets on top, then sprinkle with olive oil and salt to taste. Serve at once or chill until required.

Little Mussel Soup
Zuppetta di Cozze

This is a delicious and very simple antipasto dish which contains all the punchy flavours of the south especially, and unusually for mussels, the pungency of oregano. Please make sure the mussels are very clean and fresh. You can decorate the finished dish with the prettiest shells.

SERVES 4

1 kg (1¾ lb) fresh, live mussels in their shells

2–3 garlic cloves, chopped

1 dried red chilli pepper, chopped

4 tablespoons extra virgin olive oil

a pinch of salt

½ wine glass of dry white wine

4 thick slices of coarse Italian bread

a large pinch of dried oregano

Clean and scrub all the mussels, scraping off the beards, then rinse them well in several changes of cold fresh water. When they are clean, place them in a large pan, cover and steam over a high heat for about 8 minutes until the shells have opened. Discard any that remain closed. Remove the mussels from the pan and take them out of their shells. Strain the liquid and put it to one side.

Fry the garlic, chilli and oil for 5 minutes in another pan. Add the mussels and stir together for about 5 minutes. Season with salt, then add the wine and boil off the alcohol for 1 minute. Add the liquid from the mussels and lower the heat. Simmer gently until bubbling hot.

Toast the bread lightly on both sides, then lay the slices in the bottom of four large, warmed soup plates. Pour over the *zuppetta*, sprinkle generously with oregano and serve at once.

OLIO DI SEMI

TABELLA REGOLAMENTARE

BURRO NATURALE

TABELLA REGOLAMENTARE

PASTA TIPO O

DEC. MIN. 8-10-49 ART. 2 e 6

PANE TIPO O

DEC. MIN. 8-10-49 ART. 2 e 6

OLIO DI OLIVA

TABELLA REGOLAMENTARE

OLIO DI SEMI VARI

INSACCATI MISTI

2 First Courses

For most Italians, *i primi* has to be the most important course of their meal, the one which is most representative of the skills of the cook and the style of the household or restaurant. Italians are incredibly emotional about their food, and never more so than over the poetry generated by a perfect risotto or a memorable plate of pasta.

The first course used to mark the start of a three- or four-course meal but, as in the case of the antipasto, many people now serve only one course as their entire meal. Only very recently, when I took a group of my students out to lunch at Da Leo, one of Lucca's oldest and most typical *osterie*, the waiter himself could not contain his surprise at the amount of food my group of Australians, Americans, Hong Kong Chinese and British were ordering and consuming with such relish at every course. I reminded him, however, that they were on an eating holiday, where the only real way to study and learn is through your taste buds!

The first course will be either pasta, risotto or soup, or a perhaps a plate of gnocchi or similar dish which does not fall into any of the other categories, but is neither fish, game, poultry, seafood or meat-based. When planning a menu, it is important to bear in mind how filling the first course is going to be, especially as it is usually quite starchy. Because of this, the meat course can be light on meat and rich in vegetables, which altogether means a healthier meal that is lower in fats. On the other hand, there is nothing to stop you from skipping the first course altogether and following an antipasto with a main course, although it would be a shame to miss out on such an integral and typically Italian part of the meal!

Pappardelle with Chicken Livers
Paparele e Figadini

Pastasciutta is the Italian word which refers to a dish of pasta that is drained, tossed with a sauce and served dry apart from the sauce. An alternative first course is a soup in which pasta has been cooked: this is a *minestra* or *zuppa* with pasta. This particular Venetian speciality is a cross between the two and it relies heavily on the freshness and good quality of the chicken livers and the richness of the stock. Although the pasta is called *paparele*, which is probably the dialect for pappardelle, these thumb-width strips are not the same as the wide ribbons that are Tuscany's most traditional pasta shape.

SERVES 4

FOR THE PASTA
250 g (9 oz) plain white flour
2 eggs
2 tablespoons milk

FOR THE SAUCE
175 g (6 oz) chicken livers, trimmed, washed and dried
50 g (2 oz) unsalted butter
1.2 litres (2 pints) beef stock, kept simmering
50 g (2 oz) Parmesan cheese, freshly grated
a pinch of salt
3 tablespoons chopped fresh parsley

To make the pasta dough, pile the flour in a mound on the work top, make a hollow in the centre and break the eggs into the hollow. Mix the eggs into the flour with your fingertips, then knead with both hands. Knead for at least 10 minutes, adding the milk as you do so. Roll out the dough and cut into thumb-width strips with a sharp knife.

In a very large pan, fry the chicken livers in the butter until well browned. Add the stock and bring to the boil, then add the pasta and cook for about 3–5 minutes until just tender. Stir the Parmesan through the mixture, season with salt and serve sprinkled with the chopped parsley.

Polenta Gnocchi
Gnocchi di Polenta

This is a tremendously substantial dish which is perfect for freezing cold, damp Tuscan days after picking olives all morning, or after splitting and stacking logs. It is a real ribsticker, so if you decide to serve it make sure the next course is very light. However, one good thing is that polenta never leaves you feeling full for long, as it is quickly digested.

SERVES 4

50 g (2 oz) dried porcini mushrooms

1 large onion, thinly sliced

100 g (4 oz) unsalted butter

50 ml (2 fl oz) olive oil

300 g (11 oz) stewing pork, cubed

1 tablespoon tomato purée

150 ml (5 fl oz) pork stock

2 litres (3½ pints) cold water

a large pinch of salt

500 g (1 lb 2 oz) yellow polenta flour

5 heaped tablespoon freshly grated
   Parmesan cheese

Cover the mushrooms in warm water and let them soak for about 15 minutes. Meanwhile, fry the onion in half the butter and the olive oil until soft. Add the pork and stir together to brown the meat thoroughly all over. Stir the tomato purée into the stock, then stir the mixture into the pan. Drain the mushrooms, chop them coarsely, then stir them into the pan. Leave simmering very gently while you make the polenta.

In a separate pan, bring the cold water to a rolling boil with the salt, then trickle the polenta flour into the boiling water, whisking constantly. Stir the polenta continuously for about 45 minutes until it comes away from the sides of the pan. Tip the cooked polenta out on to a wooden board.

Preheat the oven to 200°C/400°F/gas mark 6. Butter a large ovenproof dish very thoroughly.

Using a tablespoon dipped into cold water, scoop the polenta into small balls and use them to line the bottom of the dish. Cover with some of the pork, dot with some of the remaining butter and sprinkle with Parmesan. Continue in this way, layering the polenta, meat, butter and cheese until all the ingredients have been used up. The final layer should be polenta coated in butter and cheese. Heat through in the oven for 5–10 minutes, then serve at once.

Gnocchi Disaster

Making gnocchi is never easy – anybody who tells you it is, is some kind of genius or saint. It is the easiest thing in the world if what you are trying to achieve is rubbery, bouncing, hard little balls which take a week to digest. It is very hard to make light, fluffy, perfectly shaped dumplings that taste as good as they look.

On one course in the Veneto, the whole class had spent an entire morning making beautiful potato gnocchi, not because they are necessarily part of the local repertoire of traditional dishes, but because they all wanted to learn how to do it. We then went out for the day, leaving the gnocchi in neat rows chilling in the cool room.

Upon our return, having all changed for dinner, my crew and I set about cooking the gnocchi. The sauce simmered and the salted water was brought to the boil. One by one, we dropped them into the pan. One by one, they disintegrated, coating the surface of the water with a thick scum of mashed potato. Disaster! What were we to do? This is one of the few really non-salvageable dishes! All I knew was that I had a dining room full of hungry clients and that the first course of our carefully, lovingly planned dinner was definitely now off!

With the few ingredients left at my disposal – we were due to restock and a shopping expedition with clients was scheduled as next morning's lesson – I fell back on my Roman years . . . we had *Spaghetti Aglio e Olio*, and nobody complained, though I did have to bring the most revolting-looking pot of floating mashed gnocchi to the table in order to explain the sudden change in menu. Typically, if somewhat surprisingly, some of the guests got quite emotional and insisted on tasting the ruined gnocchi despite their appearance!

Rice and Peas
Risi e Bisi

There is much discussion about the 'right' texture of a risotto. In this case, you can go for as soupy and liquid a texture as you like. I have been served this dish countless times in Venice and the surrounding areas and only once have I had it so that it could be eaten with a fork. For extra flavour, add the pods of your peas to the stock.

SERVES 4

½ mild onion, very finely chopped

50 g (2 oz) pancetta, chopped

3 tablespoons extra virgin olive oil

50 g (2 oz) unsalted butter

25 g (1 oz) fresh parsley, chopped

1 kg (2¼ lb) sweet tender young
   peas, shelled and rinsed

1 litre (1¾ pints) good-quality beef stock,
   kept simmering

300 g (11 oz) risotto rice, preferably
   Vialone Nano Gigante

salt and freshly milled black pepper

50 g (2 oz) Parmesan cheese, freshly grated,
   plus extra for serving

Gently fry the onion, pancetta, olive oil and butter for about 10 minutes in a heavy-based pan. Add the parsley, stir and fry gently for a further 4 minutes. Add the peas and stir thoroughly. Add just enough stock barely to cover the ingredients, bring to the boil, then simmer very gently for about 15 minutes until the peas begin to become tender. Stir in the rice. Add a ladleful of stock, season with salt and pepper and stir, waiting patiently for the grains to absorb the stock before you add any more. After about 20 minutes, when the rice is soft and tender and has absorbed all the stock, take the pan off the heat, stir in the Parmesan, cover and leave to rest for 3 minutes before turning on to a warmed platter to serve. Offer extra grated cheese at the table.

Dressed Polenta
Polenta Conzata

This is a deep midwinter comfort food special! Whatever cheese you choose, just make sure it is really very tasty indeed, as the polenta, being rather bland, needs strong flavours to bring it alive. Fontina is a good choice, as is Asiago or mature Provolone Piccante. Other alternatives are a good Parmigiano or Grana, or you could even melt some Gorgonzola into the polenta if you prefer. To make polenta taste less bland, try and buy polenta flour which has been recently ground and is therefore fresh. Quick-cook polenta (five minutes as opposed to 50) has improved a great deal, but shop around and experiment before you decide on your favourite brand. Sometimes I add a generous pinch of dried mixed herbs or sage to the polenta as it is cooking to make it less bland.

SERVES 4

300 ml (10 fl oz) milk

300 ml (10 fl oz) water

a pinch of salt

350 g (12 oz) polenta flour

125 g (4½ oz) unsalted butter, diced

100 g (4 oz) cheese packed with lots of flavour
 (see above), freshly grated

150 g (5 oz) fresh Ricotta cheese

To make the polenta, bring the water and milk to the boil with the salt. Slowly drizzle in the polenta and whisk until thick. Stir hard for 45–50 minutes or until cooked through. In this case, the polenta should not be too stiff. Stir the butter through the polenta. Divide the grated cheese and Ricotta between four bowls, spoon the buttered polenta on top and serve.

Venetian Bean and Pasta Soup
Pasta e Fagioli

Every single region of Italy has at least one recipe for this old and traditional household dish containing the poorest of ingredients: a handful of pasta, a few vegetables, a little fatty pork, beans and stock. It varies only a little from one place to another, but is very much representative of the peasant style of cooking in the Veneto, which sharply contrasts with the elegant dishes of the aristocracy. Just as Tuscany favours the borlotti bean, the Veneto too has its favourite variety for this dish. It is called lamon and looks very similar to borlotti, albeit slightly longer in shape. Unfortunately, you are not likely to come across it very often outside the region itself so you can use borlotti instead. If you use fresh beans in their pods, they will need to be soaked and treated like dried beans, although they cook in about 30 minutes.

SERVES 4

300 g (11 oz) dried beans, preferably lamon, soaked overnight in cold water

75 g (3 oz) fatty pancetta or prosciutto crudo

2 tablespoons olive oil

50 g (2 oz) olive oil or pork fat

1 onion, chopped

1 carrot, chopped

1 celery stick, chopped

1 litre (1¾ pints) good-quality meat stock

150 g (5 oz) tiny, rice-grain size pasta

salt and freshly milled black pepper

Drain the soaked beans, then place in a pan and cover with fresh water. Bring to the boil and boil rapidly for 5 minutes, then drain, rinse and return to the pan. Cover with fresh unsalted water and simmer for about 45 minutes until tender. Drain well.

Fry the pancetta or prosciutto and olive oil or pork fat with the onion, carrot and celery in a large pan until the vegetables are soft. Add the beans and stir thoroughly. Add the stock, bring to the boil and simmer gently for about 45–50 minutes until the beans are almost falling apart. Add the pasta and cook for about 10 minutes until just tender. Season to taste with salt and pepper and serve warm.

Giant Ravioli with Beetroot and Mascarpone
Ravioloni Rosa

I think this dish always looks so beautiful with the brilliant heliotrope pink of the beetroot spurting out from the white of the pasta, sitting in a little pool of melted butter studded with poppy seeds – and it tastes as good as it looks. It is really important not to use pickled beetroot.

SERVES 4

FOR THE FILLING

2 large beetroot, boiled <u>not</u> pickled

150 g (5 oz) Mascarpone cheese

2 tablespoons freshly grated
   Parmesan cheese

a large pinch of ground cumin

salt and freshly milled black pepper

FOR THE PASTA

400 g (14 oz) plain white flour

4 eggs

½ teaspoon extra virgin olive oil

FOR THE DRESSING

100 g (4 oz) unsalted butter

1½ teaspoons poppy seeds

Make the filling first. Drain the beetroot carefully and cool until just warm, but not cold. Peel and cube the beetroot, then process until completely smooth. Add the Mascarpone to make a smooth, quite thick purée. Stir in the Parmesan and cumin, then season to taste with salt and pepper. Chill until required.

To make the pasta, pile the flour in a mound on the work top, make a hollow in the centre and break in the eggs. Mix the eggs into the flour with your fingertips, then knead with both hands for at least 10 minutes, adding the olive oil as you do so. Then begin to roll the dough out as thinly as possible, fold it in half, roll it out again and repeat about six times. (If you have a pasta machine, roll it out to the penultimate thickness.) Cut the rolled out dough into eight sheets each about 10 x 24 cm (4 x 9½ in). Drop four spoonfuls of filling evenly along four of the sheets. Lay the four spare sheets on top and cut into four across the width, then around the edges, using a pastry wheel and sealing the edges carefully to make 16 ravioloni. Any leftover filling can be spooned over hot pasta as a dressing.

Bring a large pan of salted water (or stock) to the boil. Slide in your ravioloni and boil just until they float on the surface and the pasta is tender, about 4–5 minutes. Scoop out with a slotted spoon and arrange on four warmed plates.

Meanwhile, melt the butter until nutty but not dark brown. Stir in the poppy seeds, leave to stand for 15 minutes, then pour over each portion and serve at once.

Doge's Soup
Zuppa dei Dogi

This recipe is based on a very old one taken from the kitchens of the Doge's Palace in Venice. It is supposed to represent the beauty and glory of Venice with all the colours of precious stones; while the golden rice balls represent the real gold of her great wealth.

SERVES 6

150 g (5 oz) long-grain rice

50 g (2 oz) Fontina cheese,
  freshly grated

1 egg

25 g (1 oz) Parmesan cheese,
  freshly grated

1 tablespoon olive oil

1.5 litres (2½ pints) meat stock,
  strained

1 large beetroot, boiled, peeled
  and cut into matchsticks

1 large carrot, boiled
  and cut into matchsticks

1 large dark green courgette,
  boiled briefly, then cut into matchsticks

1 large yellow potato, peeled,
  boiled and cut into matchsticks

4–6 tablespoons plain white flour

oil for deep-frying

Cook the rice in boiling water for 10 minutes or until still quite firm, then drain. Mix the rice with the Fontina until well blended, then add the egg, Parmesan and olive oil. Mix thoroughly and shape into walnut-sized balls. Chill until required.

Bring the stock to the boil in a large pan, then add the beetroot, carrot, courgette and potato matchsticks and simmer for 5 minutes. Be very careful not to allow the vegetable matchsticks to cook any longer or they will lose their shape.

Meanwhile, coat the chilled rice balls lightly in flour and deep-fry in hot oil until golden and crisp. Drain carefully. Place the rice balls in individual, warmed soup plates and ladle over the soup. Serve at once.

Barolo Risotto
Risotto al Barolo

This is one of those rich, satisfying dishes which remind me of being fog-bound in remote corners of the rice-growing provinces of Piedmont or Lombardy. A filling dish, it needs to be followed by light courses and a long walk to work it off.

SERVES 6

200 g (7 oz) fresh or dried borlotti beans, soaked overnight in cold water

300 g (11 oz) stewing veal

2 onions

1 celery stick

1 carrot

1.2 litres (2 pints) cold water

salt and freshly milled black pepper

125 g (4½ oz) unsalted butter

500 g (1 lb 2 oz) risotto rice

2 or even 3 bottles of good Barolo

75 g (3 oz) Parmesan cheese, freshly grated

Drain and rinse the beans, then place them in a pan, cover with cold water, bring to the boil and boil rapidly for 5 minutes. Drain and rinse again, return to the pan and cover with fresh water to come 6 cm (2½ in) above the beans. Bring to the boil and simmer gently until tender but not falling apart, 20–30 minutes for fresh beans or 45–60 minutes for dried. Do not add salt until the beans are tender as it will make the skins toughen. Drain and keep to one side.

Next, make the stock. Put the meat, one onion, the celery, carrot, water and a little salt in a pan and bring to the boil. Cover and simmer gently for about 2 hours. Remove the meat and vegetables, trim the meat and chop the meat and vegetables finely. Strain the stock, season and keep simmering gently.

Now melt half the butter in a large, heavy-based pan. Chop the second onion finely and fry it in the butter until soft and golden. Add the rice and toast it quickly until it is coated in butter, shiny and hot. Add the first glass full of Barolo, stir and allow the alcohol to evaporate, then add a ladleful of hot stock, stir and allow the rice to absorb the liquid, then add more Barolo. Continue in this way until the rice is half cooked, about 10 minutes. Season to taste. Then add the beans, more wine and stock and cook for a further 4 minutes. Add the chopped meat and vegetables and continue as before until the risotto is creamy and velvety but the rice grains are still firm to the bite. Remove from the heat and add the remaining butter and all the Parmesan. Stir, cover and leave to stand for about 5 minutes before turning out on to a warmed serving platter.

Barolo Vines

October was very wet that year. We had always planned to take the group to see the first day of the Barolo harvest. This is a very significant moment for any wine producer in Piedmont, as this date, the very last one in the picking calendar, is the only one which is fixed by the regulators and not by the wine producer himself. That way, all the Nebbiolo grapes which are destined for Barolo and not one of the other wines, are picked on exactly the same day. 'But isn't that easier?' I enquired. 'How do you normally chose the day on which to start the *vendemmia*?' Wryly, Aldo Vajra, one of Piedmont's most highly respected wine makers, put his head on one side and said, shrugging, 'We just choose . . . and then later . . . we know that it was always the wrong day that we chose . . .'

The group, the driver and I sat in a van on the hillside and watched the horizontal lines of slate grey rain pour out of the sky and on to the vineyards, the road and the paths. Outside, the pickers slipped and slithered their way up and down the hillocks, carrying their precious cargo of Nebbiolo destined exclusively for Barolo, with the orange-red and white mud slicking up their legs. This is the only grape harvest in the area where the grapes are picked in tiny five-kilogram boxes and gently tipped into the waiting tractor at the side of the road. Only the south side of the hill is harvested, the east and west sides being used for other, less distinguished wines, and the north side being left for mushrooms, truffles and chestnuts. It was incredibly wet, which made it particularly difficult, but the work appeared all the more relentless and dedicated under these circumstances.

A few days later, when the rain had stopped, we went back and stood quietly by the side of the road in exactly the same spot. There are few things which can be more lovely than neat, ordered, freshly harvested vineyards on a Piedmontese hillside in soft, early autumn light, when the leaves are glowing red, yellow and bronze and the valley has an air of drowsy contentment at the end of the long, hot summer. The landscape falls away so softly, with copses of trees, patches of wild flowers and the odd house sprinkled judiciously over the slopes and hummocks. It was early afternoon and already the shadows were long. All you could hear was the bird song in the woods and the drunken, bumbling, buzzing of the few bees and wasps which had survived the downpours, gorging on the last of the decaying, shrivelled, sugar-filled grapes.

The day, the season, the course, it was all ending all too quickly, all too soon! In sombre mood we hurried off to a nearby grappa maker to fortify ourselves with the next lesson on all aspects of distillation, and against the inevitable feeling of finality which comes to us all with summer's ebb.

Piedmontese Potato Gnocchi
Gnocchi di Patate alla Piemontese

The origin of potato gnocchi is hotly contested between Piedmont and Rome, both saying that the dish belongs to their region. I only know that they need a very light touch to make. It is the easiest thing in the world to make gnocchi that are rubbery and bounceable, but it is a great art to make them so that they are light as a feather and yet hold together perfectly. The right kind of floury potato is absolutely vital, as is boiling them with their skins on. Whichever end of the country the gnocchi themselves come from, this incredibly rich, cheese dressing is totally Piedmontese.

SERVES 6

1 kg (2¼ lb) floury potatoes, scrubbed

salt

3 eggs, beaten

300 g (11 oz) plain white flour

100 g (4 oz) Parmesan cheese, freshly grated

150 g (5 oz) Fontina cheese, thinly sliced

300 ml (10 fl oz) single cream

Boil the potatoes in lightly salted water until soft, then drain and peel quickly. Press through a potato ricer twice or mash very thoroughly. Blend in the eggs and flour with your hands to make a soft dough, then roll the dough into long, thumb-thick cylinders with lightly floured hands. Cut into 4 cm (1½ in) sections and form into small, concave gnocchi shapes, pressing them against the back of a fork. You should have about 72 gnocchi. Leave them spread out on large board until you are ready to cook.

Preheat the oven to 190°C/375°F/gas mark 5.

Bring a large pan of salted water to the boil, drop in the gnocchi and allow them to cook for a few minutes until they float to the surface. Scoop them out with a slotted spoon and arrange them in a well-buttered ovenproof dish. Cover with the cheeses, then pour over the cream. Bake in the oven for about 25 minutes or until well browned. Serve at once.

Wild Mushroom Risotto
Risotto con i Funghi

At the time of writing, I can report that I have had a tremendously successful year in terms of mushroom gathering. The woods and fields where I walk with my dog, Fletch, in the Sussex countryside are filled with a rarely seen abundance, and all my mushroom-picking friends report the same level of success. Around a much-loved beech tree three weeks ago, there stood six, eight- to nine-inch tall, perfect porcini, all with large, saucer-sized tops and thick, sturdy stalks, which forced me home for a substantial knife with which to cut them. They made a tremendous risotto! I was not as successful in Tuscany this autumn, which leads me to wonder if missing summer out altogether, as we did in England this year, rather than having the hottest summer on record for 200 years, as they did in Italy, means a better crop in the long run.

SERVES 6

150 g (5 oz) mixed wild mushrooms, cleaned and coarsely chopped

1 onion, chopped

1–2 garlic cloves, chopped

1 small sprig of fresh rosemary, chopped

a pinch of dried oregano

4–5 tablespoons light olive oil

1 large glass of dry white wine

500 g (1 lb 2 oz) risotto rice

salt and freshly milled black pepper

1.2 litres (2 pints) chicken or vegetable stock, kept simmering

2–3 tablespoons single cream

TO SERVE

freshly grated Parmesan cheese (optional)

Put the mushrooms, onion, garlic, herbs and olive oil into a large, heavy-based pan. Fry gently together until the mushrooms are softened and the onion is cooked. Stir in the white wine and wait for a couple of minutes for the alcohol fumes to boil off. Stir in the rice, salt and pepper and begin the cooking process by adding a ladleful of hot stock and waiting for the rice to absorb it before you add any more, stirring thoroughly each time you add more liquid. Continue in this way for about 20 minutes until the rice is tender and all the grains are plump and fluffy. Remove from the heat, stir in the cream and cover. Leave to stand for about 3 minutes before transferring to a warmed platter and serving at once. You may offer grated Parmesan cheese separately, but it is somewhat superfluous if the mushrooms have sufficient flavour of their own.

Cannelloni with Veal and Cheese Filling
Cannelloni alla Barbaroux

This has to be the richest cannelloni recipe I have ever come across, but every mouthful is so delicious you will be wanting to make it again very soon. It doesn't use pasta for the wrapping but small pancakes, which makes it even richer. You could switch to pasta sheets instead if you prefer, in which case they need to be boiled first and laid out flat on a wet surface until required. Grana cheese is first cousin to Parmigiano, so either one will be fine to use. Prosciutto cotto is Italian for cooked ham as opposed to prosciutto crudo, which is cured ham. Any good-quality cooked ham will be fine for this recipe.

SERVES 6

300 g (11 oz) stewing veal

75 g (3 oz) unsalted butter

200 g (7 oz) prosciutto cotto

6 eggs

100 g (4 oz) Grana cheese,
   freshly grated

salt

300 ml (10 fl oz) milk

a pinch of freshly grated nutmeg

about 7 tablespoons olive oil

FOR THE BÉCHAMEL SAUCE

50 g (2 oz) unsalted butter

50 g (2 oz) plain white flour

600 ml (1 pint) cold milk

Preheat the oven to 190°C/375°F/gas mark 5.

Fry the veal quickly in about one-third of the butter until well browned. Mince finely with the prosciutto. Stir in one egg and the cheese, then season with salt. Beat the remaining eggs with the milk, a pinch of salt and the nutmeg. Grease a 10 cm (4 in) pan with a little of the olive oil and use the batter to make about six small pancakes/omelettes, frying on each side until golden. Fill the pancakes with the meat filling, then roll them up to form the cannelloni. Arrange in a well-buttered ovenproof dish.

To make the béchamel sauce, melt the butter until foaming, then add the flour and stir together quickly. Add the milk and whisk together over a low heat for about 20 minutes until the sauce has thickened and no longer has a floury aftertaste. Season with a pinch of salt.

Pour the béchamel sauce over the cannelloni, dot with the remaining butter and heat through in the oven for about 15 minutes until golden and bubbling hot. Serve at once.

Minestrone Soup
Minestrone

'**M**inestrone' actually means 'big soup', and it is designed to fill you up. Apart from the assorted vegetables, the real filling quality is provided by the beans and the pasta or rice which finish it off. I am delighted to see that fresh borlotti beans are now becoming much more widely available. Somehow they always taste more Italian than the dried or canned varieties!

SERVES 6

200 g (7 oz) fresh or dried borlotti beans, soaked overnight in cold water

1 onion, finely chopped

4 tablespoons olive oil

300 g (11 oz) mixed green vegetables, such as spinach, cabbage, Swiss chard, lettuce leaves or spring greens, chopped

2 courgettes, cubed

1 potato, peeled and cubed

1 carrot, cubed

a handful of fresh flatleaf parsley, chopped

200 g (7 oz) short stubby pasta, such as penne or conchiglie, or long-grain rice

salt and freshly milled black pepper

TO SERVE

olive oil

freshly grated Parmesan cheese

First, drain and rinse the beans, then place them in a pan, cover with cold water, bring to the boil and boil rapidly for 5 minutes. Drain and rinse again, return to the pan and cover with fresh water or stock to come 6 cm (2½ in) above the beans. Bring to the boil and simmer gently until tender but not falling apart, 20–30 minutes for fresh beans or 45–60 minutes for dried beans. Do not add salt to the water until the beans are tender otherwise the skin will shrivel and harden.

Meanwhile, fry the onion very gently in the olive oil in a large pan for about 5 minutes until soft but not browned. Add the vegetables and parsley, stir together and cook for about 5 minutes until softened. Add the beans and all their water. Add more water if necessary to maintain enough liquid to cook the vegetables and to be able to call this a soup! Bring to the boil, cover and simmer very gently for about 1½ hours, stirring frequently and topping up with liquid whenever necessary, until the vegetables are thoroughly cooked.

Add the pasta or rice and boil for about 7 minutes until tender. Season to taste with salt and pepper and serve hot, leave to cool a little and serve at room temperature, or you can even serve the soup chilled. Serve olive oil and plenty of grated Parmesan separately, for guests to sprinkle on their soup.

Fontina Soup
Fonduta

This is the Italian version of a Swiss cheese fondue, so you can serve it as a dip or use it on pasta or for risotto. It is incredibly rich and filling. When I first ate it, it was poured over a huge slab of freshly cooked, steaming polenta. It was absolutely fantastic, but I had just walked up a very steep mountainside in the hot sun of an October afternoon so I really felt I'd earned it!

SERVES 4

450 g (1 lb) Fontina cheese, cubed

1 tablespoon plain white flour or polenta flour

200 ml (7 fl oz) cold milk

4 egg yolks

100 g (4 oz) unsalted butter

TO SERVE

toasted or fried bread

grissini

polenta slices

In a deep, stainless steel pan, thoroughly mix together the cheese and flour. Cover with the milk and leave to soften for about 30 minutes.

Strain the cheese and place in the top half of a double boiler or in a heatproof bowl set over a pan of simmering water. Add the egg yolks and butter and stir continuously until the cheese has melted. Keep the heat low as the eggs must not be allowed to scramble. When it is velvety smooth and piping hot, serve in hot soup plates or bowls with slices of toasted or fried bread, grissini or polenta. You can also pour it over freshly cooked tagliatelli and bake in the oven at 200°C/400°F/gas mark 6 until golden brown on top.

Spinach Gnocchi
Malfatti

This is a different type of gnocchi to the traditional spinach version using Ricotta. In this very old Medici recipe, stale bread is used instead of the cheese. As is the case with all gnocchi, the important thing is to achieve a light and feathery finish, not a lump of green rubber. The name, which means badly made, refers to their looks, not their texture!

SERVES 6

150 g (5 oz) stale bread, crusts removed

about 250 ml (8 fl oz) milk

1.5 kg (3 lb) fresh spinach, thoroughly
   washed and tough stems removed

2 eggs, beaten

2 egg yolks

2 tablespoons single cream

150 g (5 oz) Parmesan cheese,
   freshly grated

¼ teaspoon freshly grated nutmeg

salt and freshly milled black pepper

up to 5 tablespoons plain white flour

100 g (4 oz) unsalted butter

Soak the bread in enough milk to cover for about 15 minutes.

Meanwhile, place the spinach in a large pan with just the water clinging to the leaves and steam for a few minutes until just soft, then drain and cool. Use your hands to squeeze as much water as possible out of the spinach, then chop it finely or process. Put it in a large mixing bowl and stir in the eggs and egg yolks, then the cream. Squeeze the bread as dry as possible with your hands, then mix it into the spinach with about half the Parmesan. Season to taste with freshly grated nutmeg, salt and pepper.

Bring a large pan of water to the boil. Using your fingers and a very light touch, form the spinach mixture into small dumpling shapes, using the minimum amount of flour to help you and to prevent sticking. Be really careful about not using too much flour or the gnocchi will become dreadfully rubbery. Slip them carefully, in small batches, into the boiling water. Cook them for no more than 2–3 minutes; they should be ready when they float freely on the surface of the water. Remove them from the water with a slotted spoon and arrange on a warmed serving dish. Continue in this way until they are all cooked.

Meanwhile, melt the butter until warm and golden but not browned. Pour over the *malfatti* and toss gently. Sprinkle with the remaining Parmesan and serve.

Spinach and Ricotta Crescents
Orecchioni con Ripieno di Spinaci e Ricotta

If you prefer, you can leave out the sage leaves or use another favourite herb. Alternatively, you can serve the orecchioni *in brodo* by cooking and serving them directly in a clear broth.

SERVES 6

1 kg (2¼ lb) fresh spinach, thoroughly
   washed and tough stems removed

200 g (7 oz) fresh Ricotta cheese

a pinch of freshly grated nutmeg

salt and freshly milled black pepper

175 g (6 oz) Parmesan cheese, freshly grated

6 eggs

500 g (1 lb 2 oz) plain white flour

¼ teaspoon olive oil

150 g (5 oz) unsalted butter

a few fresh sage leaves, rubbed

Make the filling first. Place the spinach, with just the water still attached to it after washing, in a large pan. Cover and cook over a medium heat for just a few minutes until wilted, then drain thoroughly and cool. When it is cool enough to handle, squeeze the cooked spinach dry in your hands, then chop it finely. Mix together the spinach and Ricotta. Add the nutmeg, salt and pepper and half the Parmesan. Blend together with one egg. Set aside until required.

Now make the pasta. Tip the flour out on to the work top and make a hollow in the centre with your fist. Break the remaining eggs into the hole. Stir the eggs into the flour, then begin to knead together. Add the olive oil and knead until you have a smooth ball of elastic dough. Roll the dough out several times until fine, silky and smooth. Divide it lengthways into 6 cm (2½ in) wide strips. Drop heaped teaspoonfuls of the filling along one half of each strip, leaving a gap of 2 cm (¾ in) between each one. Fold the strips in half, encasing the filling. Using a pastry cutter or upturned glass, cut around each section of filling to make a crescent. Seal the curved edge of each one with the prongs of a fork. Continue until all the dough has been cut. Remaining scraps of dough can be finely chopped and set aside to dry, then used in a clear broth to make a simple soup.

Bring a large pan of salted water to a rolling boil. Drop the orecchioni into the water and boil for a few minutes until they are floating on the surface and tender. Transfer carefully, using a slotted spoon, to a warmed serving dish. Meanwhile, melt the butter with the sage leaves until golden but not browned, pour over the pasta and mix carefully. Sprinkle with the rest of the cheese and serve.

Pappardelle with Mushroom Sauce
Pappardelle al Sugo di Funghi

This autumn I have been making sauces such as this one a lot as the ground near my home seems to be almost visibly sprouting wild mushrooms. When you make it, do be sure that the mushrooms have plenty of flavour. Apart from the taste, one of the best things about using wild mushrooms is that they give you this unique, slightly sticky texture which you never get with cultivated mushrooms. If you are using fresh pappardelle, they will cook in about three minutes; dried will take up to six or seven minutes. If you cannot find pappardelle, go for tagliatelle or bavette instead, but in any case use a flat ribbon shape, preferably wide.

SERVES 4

300 g (11 oz) dried or fresh porcini
  or similar full-flavoured mushrooms
½ onion, chopped
2 garlic cloves, finely chopped
4 tablespoons olive oil
4 large fresh tomatoes, peeled and
  coarsely chopped

OR **6 canned plum tomatoes,
  drained and squeezed dry**
salt and freshly milled black pepper
400 g (14 oz) thick ribbon pasta,
  such as pappardelle
2 tablespoons chopped
  fresh flatleaf parsley

If you are using dried mushrooms, soak them in hand-hot water for 20 minutes, then drain. If you are using fresh mushrooms, simply clean and slice them. Cook the onion and garlic in the olive oil for about 5 minutes, stirring frequently. Add the tomatoes and stir thoroughly. Add the mushrooms and season with salt and pepper. Cook gently, stirring occasionally, for about 40 minutes or until the sauce becomes creamy and the mushrooms very soft.

Meanwhile bring a large pan of salted water to a rolling boil. Add the pappardelle and stir. Return to the boil and simmer until *al dente*. Drain and return to the pan. Add the sauce and mix together, then transfer to a warmed serving platter, sprinkle with parsley and serve at once.

Baked Tomatoes with Rice
Pomodori Ripieni di Riso

This is another childhood-memory recipe, made when the tomatoes in the vegetable garden towards the end of summer were so sweet and ripe and wrinkled that this dish needed practically nothing else except for the rice and a little oil. I remember carrying in the tomatoes and watching them go from basket to baking tin in a matter of minutes, emerging after one short hour bursting at the seams with the rice, and with the tomato sweetened to a dense, burnt caramel by the oven's heat mixed with the magic of olive oil. The purpose of the potatoes is to keep the tomatoes in place upright, so use the slices as you see fit to wedge the tomatoes in the correct position.

SERVES 6

6 large, ripe, firm tomatoes

200 g (7 oz) long-grain rice

2 garlic cloves, finely chopped

75 ml (3 fl oz) olive oil

10 fresh basil leaves, torn into shreds

1 tablespoon dried oregano

salt and freshly milled black pepper

1 large potato, cut into 6 thick slices about the same circumference as the tomatoes

Preheat the oven to 180°C/350°F/gas mark 4.

Slice the tops off the tomatoes and set them aside. Scoop out the inside of the tomatoes and discard the seeds. Chop the flesh of the tomatoes and put it into a bowl. Add the rice, garlic, half the olive oil and the herbs. Season generously with salt and pepper and use to fill the tomatoes. Replace the lids on the tomatoes. Lightly oil an ovenproof dish with most of the remaining oil. Arrange the potato slices on the bottom of the dish and place each tomato on a slice of raw potato. Pour about 3 cm (1¼ in) of cold water around the tomatoes and potato. Pour the remaining oil on top of the tomatoes and bake in the oven for about 55 minutes or until the rice is tender and the tomatoes soft. You may need to add more water during the cooking time if the tomatoes have dried out too much for the rice to cook and swell. Serve warm or cold.

Pappardelle with Hare Sauce
Pappardelle alla Lepre

For this great autumn classic, you must begin a day ahead as the hare will need to marinate thoroughly overnight. Pappardelle are flat, wide ribbons of pasta which are traditional for this dish and to Tuscany as a whole.

SERVES 8

500 ml (17 fl oz) dry red wine	5 tablespoons olive oil
1 large onion, quartered	450 g (1 lb) streaky bacon or pancetta, chopped
1 celery stick, quartered	a large pinch of freshly grated nutmeg
5–6 peppercorns	salt and freshly milled black pepper
a pinch of dried thyme	250 ml (8 fl oz) beef or game stock
2 bay leaves	750 g (1¾ lb) plain white flour
	6 eggs
1.5 kg (3 lb) hare, jointed into 8 sections	75 g (3 oz) unsalted butter, diced

Put the wine, onion, celery, peppercorns, thyme and bay leaves into a bowl. Place the hare in the marinade, submerge it thoroughly and cover the bowl with clingfilm. Leave in a cool place to stand for about 12 hours.

Drain the hare joints thoroughly and strain the marinade. Put the olive oil and bacon or pancetta into a heavy-based pan and fry gently until the fat runs. Lay the hare joints in the pan and brown all over. Season to taste with nutmeg, salt and pepper. Cover and simmer gently for 1½ hours, gradually adding the marinade and stock alternately so the meat stays completely moist. When the meat is very tender, remove the pan from the direct heat and keep warm until required.

To make the pasta, tip the flour on to the work top and make a hollow in the centre. Break in the eggs with a pinch of salt. Stir the eggs into the flour, then knead until you have a smooth ball of elastic dough, about 10 minutes. Roll the dough out several times until silky and smooth, then cut it into strips as wide as a man's thumb and of a length which you can comfortably cook in your pan.

Heat the hare until bubbling hot while you bring a large pan of salted water to the boil. Take the joints out of the sauce, set them aside and keep them warm. Toss the pasta into the boiling water, stir, return to the boil and cook for about 3 minutes until *al dente*. Drain the pasta and return it to the empty pan. Pour over the sauce from the hare and toss thoroughly. Add the butter and toss again. Divide the pasta between warmed plates, top with the hare and serve at once.

Pappardelle with Wild Boar Sauce in the Arezzo Style

Pappardelle al Sugo di Cinghiale all'Aretina

This is my adaptation of a similar dish served at Alvaro Maccioni's restaurant La Famiglia in Langton Street, Chelsea. In the light of long discussions with my dear friend Alvaro about this recipe, I have decided that it is the judicious use of spices, the fennel seed in particular, which makes the sauce truly outstanding.

SERVES 4

1 onion, chopped

1 carrot, chopped

1 celery stick, chopped

100 g (4 oz) prosciutto crudo, chopped

4 tablespoons olive oil

450 g (1 lb) wild boar stewing steak, cubed

1 tumbler of full-bodied red wine

salt and freshly milled black pepper

5 tablespoons tomato purée

6 tablespoons hot stock

200 g (7 oz) passata

a pinch of fennel seeds

a pinch of ground cumin

400 g (14 oz) pappardelle (see page 56) or similar thick, ribbon pasta

TO SERVE

freshly grated Parmesan (optional)

Fry the vegetables gently with the prosciutto and the olive oil until the onion is transparent. Add the meat and seal on all sides until browned. Pour over the wine and bring to the boil, season with salt and pepper, cover and simmer for about 1½ hours or until the meat is completely tender.

Blend together the tomato purée and stock. While the meat continues to cook, gradually add the diluted tomato purée and the passata. Add the fennel seeds and cumin and stir thoroughly. Cover again and simmer for a further 1 hour. Check and adjust the seasoning to taste.

Bring a large pan of salted water to a rolling boil, add the pappardelle, stir and return to the boil. Boil for about 3 minutes for fresh or 7 minutes for dried until the pasta is *al dente*. Drain well, then return to the empty pan. Pour over the sauce and mix together thoroughly, then transfer to a warmed serving platter or individual plates and serve with the Parmesan offered separately, if liked.

Baked Courgette Mould
Tortino di Zucchine

The best way to marry the flavours of fresh, ripe, summer tomatoes with the flavour of courgettes, this recipe makes a really good main-course dish or a fairly substantial first-course dish.

SERVES 6

8–10 medium to large
  courgettes, sliced lengthways
  into thick 'tongues'
about 1 tablespoon salt
4 tablespoons plain white flour
250 ml (8 fl oz) sunflower oil
1 onion, chopped

3 tablespoons olive oil
750 g (1¾ lb) ripe, summer tomatoes,
  peeled, seeded and coarsely chopped
8 fresh basil leaves, torn into shreds
a large pinch of dried oregano
salt and freshly milled black pepper
150 g (5 oz) Mozzarella cheese,
  finely chopped

Lay the courgette 'tongues' in a colander. Sprinkle with salt and cover with a plate. Weigh the plate down with a couple of tins and stand the colander in a sink to drain for about 2 hours.

Rinse and dry the courgettes, then toss lightly in plain flour. Heat the sunflower oil until a small piece of bread dropped into the oil sizzles instantly. Fry the courgettes until golden brown, then drain thoroughly on kitchen paper. Fry the onion in the olive oil, then add the tomatoes, basil and oregano. Stir together thoroughly and season with salt and pepper. Cover and simmer for about 30 minutes, then rub the sauce through a sieve.

Preheat the oven to 180°C/350°F/gas mark 4.

Cover the bottom of an ovenproof dish with a layer of the sauce. Cover with a layer of fried courgettes, then with a layer of Mozzarella. Continue in this way until all the ingredients have been used up, finishing with courgettes and Mozzarella. Bake in the oven for about 20 minutes until heated through and bubbling.

Tomato and Bread Soup
Pappa al Pomodoro

In the 1960s, there was a hit record in Italy called 'La Pappa al Pomodoro' in which the singer, Rita Pavone, repeated the words 'Viva la pappa al pomodoro' over and over again as part of the chorus. It was weird even then! Anyway, this is a thick soup which makes the best of the glut of over-ripe tomatoes at the end of a Tuscan summer, and that ever-present standby ingredient, stale bread. It tastes marvellous served lukewarm with plenty of basil and extra olive oil for the diners to drizzle over the top.

SERVES 6

1.5 litres (2½ pints) vegetable, chicken or meat broth

1 onion, chopped

1.25 kg (2½ lb) very ripe, soft tomatoes, coarsely chopped

8 tablespoons olive oil

400 g (14 oz) stale bread, crusts removed and thinly sliced

3 garlic cloves, crushed

a handful of fresh basil leaves, chopped

salt and freshly milled black pepper

Heat the broth slowly in a large pan. Meanwhile, put the onion, tomatoes and half the olive oil in a separate pan and fry together over a gentle heat for about 10 minutes until soft. Push the mixture through a food mill or sieve and add it to the hot broth. Add the bread, garlic and basil and season to taste with salt and pepper. Cover and simmer gently for about 45 minutes until thick and creamy, stirring occasionally. Stir in the remaining oil, adjust the seasoning and serve.

Tagliolini in Lemon Butter
Tagliolini al Limone

I believe any shape of pasta is suitable for this sauce, although it has to be said that back in Menfi, hand-made tagliolini tasted just perfect. Tagliolini are thin strips of pasta about half the width of tagliatelle. This is a pasta sauce that depends entirely on the quality of the lemons.

SERVES 4

50 g (2 oz) unsalted butter

rind of 2 unwaxed lemons

50 g (2 oz) Parmesan or
  Pecorino cheese, freshly grated

freshly milled black pepper

FOR THE PASTA

250 g (9 oz) plain white flour

2 eggs

Melt the butter very gently with the lemon rind and leave to infuse for at least 2 hours. Discard the lemon rind.

To make the pasta, pile the flour in a mound on the work top, make a hollow in the centre and break the eggs into the hollow. Mix the eggs into the flour with your fingertips, then knead with both hands. Knead for about 10 minutes until the dough is smooth and soft. Roll out as thinly as possible and cut into thin ribbons.

Bring a large pan of salted water to the boil, toss in the pasta and stir. Return to the boil and cook for about 3–5 minutes until just tender. Drain the pasta, reserving a little of the cooking water. Toss the pasta with the lemon butter, cheese, pepper and a little of the reserved cooking water if the dish looks too dry.

An alternative sauce can be made by warming 250 ml (8 fl oz) of single cream, stirring in the infused butter and the juice of one lemon and using this creamy sauce to dress the pasta.

Making Fresh Pasta in Sicily

It was September in western Sicily, and we were into the second day of the course. We were running two courses back to back – in other words we would have less than 24 hours to clear up and be ready to start again once the first week's group had left to return home. Every course I teach always begins with a two-hour lecture on the local ingredients, with all the ingredients we are likely to use in the course of the week laid out on a table as a gorgeous still life. Having given a theoretical introduction to what lies in store, we move on to the first practical hands-on lesson, which is always making fresh pasta.

The reason I choose this is because it is a fun lesson which requires very few ingredients, and because the general mess of flour and eggs is a great ice-breaker. Also, several people will either have made or attempted to make it before, so there are many different levels of expertise. The other reason is that pasta is universally liked, and is so representative of Italy's kitchen.

On the first week, it was about 43 degrees Celsius, with rain falling in sheets and an intense and oppressive humidity. We tried not to be daunted, however, and kept cooling fans whirring busily in appropriate places. After the pasta has been kneaded and rolled out, it needs to rest a little before it can be cut into the required shape. Normally, in the dry heat of Sicily, this takes only a couple of minutes, but on this occasion, the humidity meant that all attempts at cutting tagliatelle, spaghetti, *capelli d'angelo*, *malfatti*, *garganelli* or anything else just resulted in moist, lumpy, heaps of stubborn goo.

The dinner hour was fast approaching and I felt myself beginning to worry about what we were going to do next. Then – a brilliant inspiration – I sent all the ladies back upstairs to their rooms to get their hairdryers! Success! We managed to dry out the pasta perfectly, using up a great deal of electricity, and soon heaps of every conceivable shape of fresh pasta were lying neatly on clean trays waiting to be cooked and enjoyed. Dinner was a huge success and was accompanied by the usual incredulity of all the cooks: 'did we really make this ourselves?'

The following week, the temperature remained exactly the same but the rain clouds moved off elsewhere and within an hour Sicily was back to that relentless, baking, scorching, dry heat that has been synonymous with this glorious island for

thousands of years. This did not make for a particularly pleasant clear-up and set-up session as we waved one group off at the airport and welcomed the next – but worse was to come.

In the pasta class, it was now nigh on impossible to prevent the pasta from drying out in the parching heat. All attempts at cutting the pasta just resulted in small, shapeless bits of shattered, completely dry pasta littering the floor. The only way round the problem was to work incredibly quickly so as to prevent it from drying out before we could cut it. This was a lot to ask in the incredible heat, especially working in a kitchen with ten others, so I am only glad that the extreme conditions meant that nobody was terribly hungry anyway, and therefore the distinct lack of pasta on the table that night came as more of a relief than anything else!

Pasta with Fresh Sardines
Pasta con le Sarde

I like to go out and pick the wild fennel which grows so luxuriously everywhere on this beautiful island; the picking is part of the whole ritual of making this great Sicilian classic. To eat this dish is to understand something quintessentially Sicilian. If you are not lucky enough to be in Sicily, you can use fennel tops.

SERVES 6

150 g (5 oz) wild fennel leaves
   and stalks, washed and
   carefully trimmed
2 teaspoons fine salt
2 litres (3½ pints) water
1 large onion, chopped
1 sachet of saffron powder
3 tablespoons cold water
6–7 tablespoons olive oil

40 g (1½ oz) pine kernels
40 g (1½ oz) sultanas, soaked in warm water
   for 15 minutes, then drained
300 g (11 oz) fresh sardines, gutted, boned and headless
2 salted anchovies, boned and rinsed
salt and freshly milled black pepper
400 g (14 oz) long pasta, such as bucatini
   or thick perciatelli

TO SERVE

crusty bread

Put the fennel in a large pan with the salt and water. Bring to the boil, cover and simmer for about 10 minutes. Remove the fennel, drain and squeeze dry, then chop very finely. Reserve all the water as it will be used to cook the pasta.

Put the onion in a large pan and cover generously with water. Simmer for about 10 minutes until the onion is soft. Dilute the saffron in the cold water, then add to the pan with about half the olive oil, the pine kernels and the drained sultanas. Simmer together for about 10 minutes, stirring frequently. Stir in the chopped fennel and the sardines and cover the pan. Simmer very gently for about 15 minutes, turning the fish over frequently.

In a separate pan, cook the anchovies in the remaining olive oil, mashing them into a smooth brown purée. When the sardines are cooked through, add the anchovy purée to the sardines, mix together all the ingredients and season to taste with salt and pepper. Keep warm until the pasta is cooked.

Bring a large pan of salted water to the boil, toss in the pasta and stir. Return to the boil and cook for about 7 minutes until just tender. Drain the pasta, transfer to a warmed bowl, pour over the sauce, toss thoroughly and serve hot, although the dish is possibly even better served cold the next day.

Almond Pesto with Bavette
Pesto Trapanese con le Bavette

A delicious and very different kind of pesto, this is not only marvellous with pasta, but is especially delicious when used as a stuffing inside chicken breasts, which can then be brushed with olive oil and roasted or grilled. It is also very good as a stuffing inside mackerel or other firm-fleshed fish which take kindly to being baked.

SERVES 6	**150 g (5 oz) blanched almonds, roughly chopped**
6 garlic cloves	**4 ripe tomatoes, peeled and chopped**
1 teaspoon salt	**6 tablespoons olive oil**
a large handful of fresh	**freshly milled black pepper**
basil leaves	**500 g (1 lb) bavette or spaghetti**

In a large mortar, pound the garlic, salt and basil into a paste. Gradually add the almonds and then the tomatoes. When all the ingredients are reduced to a pulp, add the oil and the pepper. If you use an electric blender, add the oil at the beginning.

Bring a large pan of salted water to the boil, toss in the pasta and stir, then cook for about 7 minutes until *al dente*. Drain the pasta and toss with the pesto in a warmed serving bowl until evenly blended. Serve at once.

Pasta with Chick Peas
Pasta e Ceci

Avery ancient recipe, some say this is the earliest recorded pasta recipe going right back to the times of the Roman legionaires, who apparently made a version of this dish at their encampments over a fire using millet flour and garam. If you don't like the flavour of anchovies or chillies, leave them out and just add the oil and garlic to the soup. It is a very chunky, thick, substantial soup which should be enjoyed with plenty of crusty bread and red wine.

SERVES 6

300 g (11 oz) dried chick peas,
    soaked overnight in cold water

9 garlic cloves, chopped to a purée

9 tablespoons olive oil, plus extra
    for serving

1.5 litres (2½ pints) water

2 x 5 cm (2 in) sprigs of fresh rosemary

salt and freshly milled black pepper

6 salted anchovies, boned, rinsed
    and very finely chopped

2 tablespoons tomato purée

300 g (11 oz) short, stubby pasta,
    such as cannolicchi or ave marie

Drain and rinse the chick peas thoroughly, then place in a pan and cover with plenty of cold water. Bring to the boil and boil rapidly for 5 minutes, then drain and rinse again. Set aside for the moment.

In a large, deep pan, fry half the garlic with about one-third of the olive oil for about 5 minutes. Add the chick peas and stir together thoroughly. Pour in the water and add the rosemary. Bring to the boil, stir and season with salt and pepper. Cover and simmer for about 1 hour or until the chick peas are soft and slightly mushy.

Meanwhile, put the remaining garlic and olive oil in a separate small pan with the anchovies and the tomato purée. Fry together very gently for about 5 minutes, stirring frequently. When the mixture is cooked through and perfectly amalgamated, remove from the heat but keep warm.

When the chick peas are cooked, add the pasta to the pan. Check that there is still sufficient liquid to cook it properly, adding a little hot water if necessary. Cook the pasta for about 7 minutes until just tender, then stir in the anchovy and garlic mixture and remove from the heat. Transfer the soup into individual bowls and coat the surface of each one with a drizzle of extra olive oil and a small sprinkling of freshly ground black pepper.

Timbale of Pasta
Timballo di Maccheroni al Ragu

This has to be the ultimate special-occasion dish, a true three or four-day event (if you count the shopping time) in order to create a really spectacular finish. I can guarantee that if you follow the instructions carefully all the way through, you will end up with a really amazing dish which has its origins buried deep in Sicilian history. This is my version of the 'Timballo del Gattopardo', the Prince of Lampedusa's own timbale, created in his honour. It is a complicated recipe, so it has been divided into sections which make it quite manageable.

SERVES 6

FOR THE RAGOUT

300 g (11 oz) veal loin, cubed

500 g (1 lb 2 oz) pork loin, cubed

500 g (1 lb 2 oz) pork ribs

100 g (4 oz) lard, chopped

1 onion, chopped

2 garlic cloves, chopped

50 g (2 oz) prosciutto crudo, finely chopped

50 g (2 oz) pork dripping

3 tablespoons olive oil

2 tablespoons chopped fresh parsley

5 large fresh basil leaves

2 dried bay leaves

2.5 cm (1 in) sprig of fresh rosemary

2.5 cm (1 in) sprig of fresh marjoram

2 cloves

½ teaspoon ground cinnamon

salt and freshly milled black pepper

250 ml (8 fl oz) dry red wine

400 ml (14 fl oz) tomato purée

4 tablespoons water

First, make the ragout. In a large flameproof casserole over the lowest possible simmering heat, place the meat, lard, onion, garlic, prosciutto, dripping, olive oil and all the herbs and spices. Season generously with salt and pepper and stir everything together very thoroughly. Partially cover and leave to cook for about 2 hours until the onion is slightly browned.

Begin very gradually to add the wine, allowing each little bit to boil off its alcohol before adding more. When all the wine has been added and the mixture is heated through and well stirred, remove all the meat with a slotted spoon and put it to one side. Raise the heat under the casserole. Add the tomato purée and stir it thoroughly into the fat and oil remaining in the casserole. Allow it to cook for about 10 minutes, stirring frequently, until it has gone very dark brown, then add the water and stir again. Cover and simmer very gently for about 2 hours.

Remove any bones from the meat, return the meat to the casserole and continue

to simmer it very gently for a further 2½ hours. During this time, you may need to skim the fat off the surface from time to time, and you may occasionally need to add a tiny amount of water. Stir it frequently whilst it cooks. When it is completely cooked through, dark brown and very thick, let it cool completely. Skim off any further surface fat once it is cold and leave the ragout in the fridge until you need it.

FOR THE PASTRY

400 g (14 oz) plain white flour

200 g (7 oz) caster sugar

225 g (8 oz) unsalted butter, diced

4 egg yolks

¼ teaspoon salt

To make the pastry, tip the flour out on to the work top and make a hollow in the centre with your fist. Put the sugar, butter, egg yolks and salt into the hollow and knead everything together using the prongs of a fork for as long as possible, then use your fingers to press it into a ball of dough. If you work this pastry too much, it will lose its marvellous crumbly texture, so only knead it for as much as you need to. Wrap the pastry in clingfilm or a plastic bag and put it in the fridge to rest for 1 hour.

Very thoroughly grease a 23 cm (9 in) diameter, 12 cm (5 in) deep mould, then dust it lightly with plain flour. Roll out two-thirds of the dough. Cut out a circle to line the base of the mould and a strip to line the sides, pressing them together gently at the seam. Put the mould back in the fridge until required. Wrap the remaining dough in clingfilm or a plastic bag and keep chilled ready to make the lid for the mould.

FOR THE MEATBALLS

200 g (7 oz) minced beef

75 g (3 oz) dried breadcrumbs

25 g (1 oz) Parmesan cheese,
  freshly grated

2 eggs

1 tablespoon chopped
  fresh parsley

600 ml (1 pint) sunflower oil
  for deep-frying

Next, make the meatballs. Knead the meat, half the breadcrumbs, the grated Parmesan, egg, parsley and some salt and pepper together to make a tasty meatball mixture. Shape into meatballs about the size of chestnuts. Beat the second egg thoroughly. Roll the meatballs first in the egg and then in the remaining breadcrumbs. Heat the oil until a small piece of bread dropped into the oil sizzles instantly. Fry all the meatballs until golden and crisp, then drain on kitchen paper until required.

FOR THE FILLING

25 g (1 oz) dried porcini mushrooms,
   soaked in boiling water for 1 hour

250 g (9 oz) Italian pork sausages

2 tablespoon pork dripping

4 tablespoons dry white wine

1 onion, thinly sliced

50 g (2 oz) pancetta, chopped

250 g (9 oz) shelled fresh or frozen peas

500 g (1 lb 2 oz) long pasta,
   such as bucatini or mezzanelli

150 g (5 oz) Parmesan cheese, freshly grated

2 hard-boiled eggs, shelled and sliced

200 g (7 oz) Mozzarella cheese, cut into discs

Now make the filling. Drain the mushrooms carefully and reserve the water. Strain the water through muslin to remove any trace of woodland undergrowth and then use enough of this water to cook the mushrooms for about 10 minutes in a small pan until completely soft. Chop them finely and set them to one side.

Pierce the sausages all over with a needle, then fry them with half the dripping on all sides for about 15 minutes until browned and cooked through. Pour over half the white wine and allow the alcohol to burn off. Remove the sausages from the pan, slice into discs and set aside. Pour their juices into the ragout.

Fry the onion and pancetta in the rest of the dripping until soft. Add the remaining wine and allow the alcohol to burn off for 1 minute before adding the peas. Cover and simmer for about 10–15 minutes until the peas are cooked, then add the mushrooms, the slices of sausage and the meatballs. Add 4 tablespoons of the ragout to this mixture and stir it all together very thoroughly. Simmer over a low heat, stirring frequently, for about 10 minutes. Leave to cool.

Bring a pan of salted water to the boil, toss in the pasta and cook for about 3 minutes until just *al dente*. Drain and return to the pan. Add one-third of the remaining ragout and toss thoroughly. Add half the Parmesan and toss again.

Preheat the oven to 190°C/375°F/gas mark 5.

Use some of the pasta to cover the bottom of the pastry-lined mould. Begin to fill the mould in layers with the ragout, the pea and sausage filling, the hard-boiled eggs, the Mozzarella and the remaining Parmesan. You can use the ingredients in whatever order you like, as long as you make sure there are lots of different layers. Press each layer down with the back of a spoon to make it all fit! When the mould is full, bang it down firmly but gently to allow it to settle. Roll out the remaining dough to make a lid and lay it on top of the mould. Pinch the edges securely closed all the way around. Pierce the top with a needle in a few places to allow the steam to escape. Bake in the oven for about 20 minutes until golden brown. Take it out of the oven and leave it to rest for 10 minutes. Carefully turn out on to a warmed serving plate and serve warm or at room temperature.

3 Main Courses

The Italian name for the main course, *il secondo*, immediately relegates the whole thing to the second division and strips it of the same degree of importance that the title 'main course' imparts. It is with this course that the deep differences in attitude towards food in general – born out of separate cultures with contrasting traditions and age-old, entrenched ideas – really comes to light when comparing Italian eating to the Anglo-Saxon habits of the table.

Every time I teach a cookery course, I spend a great deal of time listening to my students, trying to adapt the week's course to what they want and need. The request I receive most often is for 'more meat'. Gentle probing and a reflective analysis always leads me back to the same point. It is not really a lack of meat – for in various forms meat is very much present – it is actually the 'meat and two veg' scenario which is missed. 'It is all very well,' they say, 'to teach all this soup, pasta, sauces, desserts, risotto, bread, pizza, gnocchi and so on. What about the classic meat dishes? And as a totally committed carnivore, who adores nothing better than succulent, rare beef on the bone, I am only too happy to comply.

So as you can see from the following collection of recipes – which make up a part of the dishes I choose to put on the syllabus, dependent upon location and season – there is plenty here to satisfy their demands. What follows is, therefore, a mixture of the classics such as Squid Cooked in Their Own Ink (see page 79) through to Rabbit with Olives (see page 111). However, I know in my heart that the next time I casually ask, about one-third of the way through the week, whether there are any complaints and does anybody want to make suggestions, somebody is going to say 'more meat'.

Incidentally, I also have a lot of vegetarians on my courses. Recently one couple had flown all the way from Mauritius, where they live on a beach, to attend a course. This section also contains vegetarian main-course dishes, and I do strive to accommodate all vegetarians and their needs, as I feel one should at least respect their choice, even if one doesn't really understand it!

Squid Casserole with Spices
Seppie in Umido

As with the next recipe, Squid Cooked in Their Own Ink, you can add some new potatoes or slices of old potatoes to the stew for the last 30 minutes of cooking to add bulk and make the dish more substantial. I first discovered this dish when making my television series for BBC2 in 1989. Over the years I have gradually adapted it and made it my own, but it is still a great favourite and a good way to remember those heady days in Chioggia! You can serve the dish with grilled or fried polenta, as a topping for crostini, with a plain risotto made with fish stock or on a bed of garlic-flavoured mashed potatoes.

SERVES 6

4 tablespoons sunflower oil

1 large onion, chopped

2 garlic cloves, chopped

1 sprig of fresh rosemary, leaves removed and finely chopped

1 kg (2¼ lb) squid, cleaned and sliced into rings (see page 79)

500 ml (17 fl oz) cold water

200 g (7 oz) canned tomatoes, seeded and chopped

1 teaspoon tomato purée

a pinch of ground cinnamon

a pinch of freshly grated nutmeg

a pinch of ground ginger

salt and freshly milled black pepper

Heat the oil and fry the onion and garlic until soft and golden. Add the rosemary, then the squid and mix together, then cover with the water. Bring to the boil, then simmer for 45 minutes.

Add the tomatoes, tomato purée, spices, salt and pepper. Cover and simmer gently for a further 45 minutes until the squid is very tender and the sauce has thickened. Serve hot.

Inky Fingers

The fish market at Sciacca is a tumultuous gathering of vociferous fishermen, Sicilian to a man, who are there for the entirely reasonable purpose of getting the best possible price for their haul. There is very little that is either picturesque, romantic or sentimental about the building or its tenants, yet I have always felt rather fond of it and of its counterparts that are scattered all over the country, wherever there are fish and fishermen wishing to sell their catch.

The thing about letting a group of foreigners loose in such a place is that they are not necessarily one hundred per cent sure about what they are bidding for and how much money they will need to part with once they have got over their excitement. However, it must be very liberating to find oneself bidding for a box of glistening, fresh sardines, only a few hours after departing from a deeply grey London landscape. It is likely, if a touch gruesome, to conclude that the fish were still going about their daily sardine-like business at the moment when the pilot asked his crew to take their seats for landing.

At the end of a session in the fish market, we have always returned laden with boxes of sardines, squid, beef-red slices of swordfish and whatever else looked good at the time. It is the squid which have always caused the most difficulties. Somehow, most people can get over the obstacle of gutting fish, but cleaning and removing the ink sac from a squid is generally a job for the most stout-hearted. This is, incidentally, followed on the scale of 'yuck!' by the gutting and boning of a fresh sardine, which is complicated but not really unpleasant if the sardine is as fresh as the ones described above. (What is seriously unpleasant and very high on my personal 'yuck!' scale is the gutting and cleaning of a chicken.)

In order for my students to perform the indelicate and messy job of removing all that needs to be removed from the squid, including putting the intact ink sac in a separate bowl for specific dishes, I have always provided those thin latex gloves normally reserved for those occasions when a voice whose face you cannot see properly and whose hands are very much out of your line of vision, says something about things being either cold or not hurting too much. So the most fastidious don the latex, and the rest of us simply get on with the job.

It is hard not to enjoy doing this when you are sitting under a pergola of twisting, perfumed vines in a marble-flagged courtyard. The memories of these occasions are the sort of thoughts that can make me smile no matter how bad a day it might be in grim, mid-February British conditions. Imagine the expression on the face of a beef-fearing, salt-denied, shellsuit-clad Californian, struggling bravely with a small, wet, lilac and white, lumpy bit of rubber with tentacles that either spring apart or hang limply, depending upon which way up you hold it, vainly attempting to extract what looks like a well-used piece of liquorice-flavoured chewing gum without destroying the

whole thing and thus inevitably encountering the wrath of those who wish to cook it. She has a glass of wine at her elbow, is surrounded by chattering companions from all over the world, and overhead, high above in a sky streaked with heliotrope and violet from the setting sun, swallows dip and squeal.

It is a great, glorious, wonderful memory which I file away with so many others of a similar nature, and which I share with the very people who make up those memories, wherever they are now, whatever they are doing, whichever one of those recipes they might decide to cook. It is amazingly comforting to know that these memories are the ties that will always bind us, and the stories woven around the people, the recipe and the event will become part of the folklore of more than one circle of family and friends. It only takes the decision to cook a certain dish, and in the time it takes for your hand to grip the handle of the saucepan, to crush the garlic, chop the parsley, zest the lemon, the memories come flooding back just as the aroma wafts through your kitchen. The scientists are right: there is nothing as evocative as the senses of smell and taste.

Squid Cooked in Their Own Ink
Seppie col Nero

I like to add a few new potatoes to this stew for extra bulk and to tone down the flavour of the fishy black ink a little. Add the potatoes about 30 minutes from the end of the cooking time and add enough water or fish stock to allow them to cook until tender. Any of the serving suggestions in the previous recipe, Squid Casserole with Spices, will work equally well for this dish.

SERVES 4

750 g (1¾ lb) very young, small squid with ink sacs

2 garlic cloves, chopped

50 ml (2 fl oz) extra virgin olive oil

½ wine glass of dry white wine

salt and freshly milled black pepper

2 tablespoons chopped fresh parsley

You will often be able to buy squid ready prepared, either fresh or frozen. If you cannot find it, however, here's what to do. Pull off and discard the head and all the innards out of the body sac, reserving the ink sac. Using sharp scissors, cut off the tentacles and discard the sharp beak from the centre. Wash the body sac and tentacles, discarding the plastic-like quill and removing the membrane from the outside of the sac. Cut off the two side fins. The body sac, fins and tentacles are all ready for use. Cut the body sac into rings or strips.

Fry the garlic in the olive oil until soft. Add the squid pieces and seal them on all sides. Add the wine, partially cover and simmer for 45 minutes. If the pan appears dry, add a little water.

Add the ink from the sacs, partially cover and cook for a further 45 minutes or until tender. Season to taste with salt and pepper, sprinkle with the chopped parsley and serve warm.

Dried Salt Cod in the Vicenza Style
Baccalà alla Vicentina

It is essential to remove all the bones before cooking the fish. It is a very strong-tasting dish which looks quite messy when it comes to serving, as the fish sort of collapses and there is a lot of liquid. Serving it with polenta helps to improve the appearance a great deal. I like to make the polenta quite soft and serve it on individual soup plates. I make a hollow in the middle of the polenta and spoon the *baccalà* into the hollow, then sprinkle it with some freshly chopped parsley just before serving. This is one example of where the blandness of polenta works really well to offset the salty strength of the fish.

SERVES 8

1 kg (2¼ lb) dried salt cod

4 salted anchovies, boned and rinsed

a handful of fresh parsley

500 g (1 lb 2 oz) onions, chopped

2 garlic cloves, chopped

750 ml (1¼ pints) extra virgin olive oil

salt and freshly milled black pepper

6 tablespoons plain white flour

6 tablespoons freshly grated
   Parmesan cheese

500 ml (17 fl oz) milk

TO SERVE

Basic Polenta (see page 123)

Soak the cod in cold water for at least two days, changing the water twice a day, until the cod has softened. Rinse it thoroughly in cold running water, remove the skin and all the bones. You must end up with two even-sized, flat halves.

Preheat the oven to 160°C/325°F/gas mark 3.

Chop the anchovies and parsley together. Fry the onions and garlic in half the olive oil until soft, then add the anchovy and parsley mixture, stir well and remove from the heat. Spread half the fried mixture over half the fish, season with salt and pepper and sandwich the two halves together, squeezing them closed. Mix together the flour and Parmesan. Cut the filled fish into large chunks about 5 cm (2 in) square and roll each 'sandwich' in the flour and cheese mixture. Lay each section in a large ovenproof dish and cover with the remaining fried mixture, the milk and the remaining olive oil. The fish must be completely submerged. Cover and cook in the oven for 4–5 hours. Do not stir, but occasionally shake the dish and add a little more water during cooking if necessary. Serve hot with slices of grilled polenta.

Guinea Fowl with Red Wine
Faraona al Vino Rosso

Guinea fowl is a lovely bird, perfect for people who are not all that sure about game; it has just enough of a 'ripe' flavour. If you cannot find any, or would prefer to steer clear of gamey flavour altogether, the same dish works extremely well with a free-range chicken that is not too large. For a larger chicken, just use more of all the other ingredients accordingly. I have also used quail, pigeon and partridge very successfully when they have been available.

SERVES 4

1 oven-ready guinea fowl

15 g (½ oz) dried porcini
    mushrooms

200 g (7 oz) shallots
    or baby onions, chopped

50 g (2 oz) pork fat, chopped

50 g (2 oz) unsalted butter

1 tablespoon plain white flour

1 litre (1¾ pints) best-quality red wine

4 tablespoons grappa

a pinch of freshly grated nutmeg

salt and freshly milled black pepper

1 Luganega sausage, chopped

TO SERVE

Basic Polenta (see page 123)

Wipe and check over the guinea fowl. Joint it and set aside. Put the mushrooms in a cup of warm water to soak. Fry the onions with the pork fat and half the butter until the onions are soft. Lay the guinea fowl in the onions and seal all over, then sprinkle with flour and turn the pieces several times until the flour disappears. Pour over the wine and the grappa and stir thoroughly. Add the nutmeg and season with salt and pepper. Bring to the boil and boil for about 2 minutes, then reduce the heat, partially cover and simmer for about 1 hour until tender.

When the guinea fowl is cooked, take the joints out of the pan and set aside in a warm place. Boil the sauce until it has reduced by one-third, then drain the mushrooms and add them to the pan with the sausage. Cook together for about 15 minutes until the sauce is thickened and the sausage cooked through. Pour over the guinea fowl and serve with grilled polenta.

Liver Cooked in the Venetian Style
Fegato alla Veneziana

The secret to this magnificent dish is the perfection of the mashed potato. In Italy, mashed potato is made by boiling potatoes until very soft in half milk and half water, then pushing them through a food mill or mouli twice or three times. The only possible alternative is to use a potato ricer, although you will not get the same whipped-cream texture. The very briefly cooked, perfectly pink calves' liver, on its raft of caramelized red onions, can then splurge itself over the peaks and troughs created by the sublime heap of mash. This is a fantastic dish which needs no dressing up. Just don't overcook the liver!

SERVES 4

500 g (1 lb 2 oz) calves'
  or lambs' liver, very thinly sliced

750 g (1¾ lb) red onions,
  very thinly sliced

a handful of fresh parsley,
  finely chopped

3 tablespoons vegetable oil

25 g (1 oz) unsalted butter

1 wine glass of dry white wine

salt and freshly milled
  black pepper

TO SERVE

mashed potatoes (see above)

Trim the liver with care, pulling off the transparent, rind-like skin from around each slice. Rinse the onions in cold, running water, then drain and pat dry. Fry the onions and parsley gently in the vegetable oil and butter over a very low heat for 1 hour, covered, until shiny and soft. Stir frequently to avoid the onions sticking or burning. Raise the heat and lay the liver slices in the onions. Brown quickly on both sides and pour the wine over it as it browns. The liver will cook in 3 minutes. Season well with salt and pepper. Remove the liver from the pan. Tip the onions on to a warmed serving platter, arrange the liver on top and serve at once, with fluffy mashed potato.

Pork Cooked in Milk
Maiale al Latte

By the time the pork has been marinated and then slowly stewed in milk, the final texture should be almost like a baked apple: soft and juicy enough to slice through with a spoon. It really is worth using free-range, best-quality pork as you will end up with a much thicker sauce with a better consistency. It is not the more expensive cut of meat which will make the difference, just better-quality meat to start with! I prefer to make this with a hand of pork, which is always tasty, and I serve a thin prune and apple sauce on the side, finished off with grated lemon and orange zest.

SERVES 4

1 kg (2¼ lb) boned pork loin
   or leg, tied with string
500 ml (17 fl oz) dry white wine
50 g (2 oz) unsalted butter

5 sage leaves
5 tiny sprigs of fresh rosemary
salt and freshly milled black pepper
1 litre (1¾ pints) milk

Put the meat in a non-metallic bowl, cover with the wine and leave to marinate for between 6 hours and 2 days.

Remove the meat from the marinade and pat dry. Melt the butter with the herbs in a pan, add the meat and seal it until browned all over, then season with salt and pepper. Transfer the meat to a flameproof casserole and cover with the milk. Bring to the boil, cover and simmer gently for about 3 hours until the pork is tender. Remove the lid at the end and boil to let the liquid reduce for about 5 minutes. Set the meat on a warmed platter, slice thickly, and pour the sauce over the top.

Stuffed Cabbage Leaves
Rambasici

The basic principle of this dish crops up all around Italy in slightly different forms. In certain parts of Tuscany, for instance, it is sometimes called '*uccelli scappati*', which means 'escaping birds'; try to visualize small birds hiding under vegetation to get away from the hunter's gun! Whatever it is called, it is a great way of using the tough outer leaves of a cabbage. You can vary the stuffing according to what is available. I have had great success with either fish and potato, cracked wheat with mixed vegetables, sausages or cheese and potato.

SERVES 4–6

1 medium **Savoy cabbage**

300 g (11 oz) lean minced pork

300 g (11 oz) lean minced beef

50 g (2 oz) fresh parsley, chopped

2 garlic cloves, finely chopped

2 hard-boiled eggs, shelled
and finely chopped

2 slices of brown bread,
cut into very small cubes

2–3 slices of salami, cut into small squares

paprika

salt and freshly milled black pepper

6 tablespoons vegetable or sunflower oil

OR 4 tablespoons unsalted butter

1 large onion, sliced

300 ml (10 fl oz) meat stock, warm

1 heaped tablespoon dried breadcrumbs

1 heaped tablespoon freshly grated
Parmesan cheese

2 tablespoons olive oil

Select about 12 large outer leaves of the cabbage. Bring a large pan of water to the boil, add the leaves and blanch for 1 minute, then drain well and pat dry.

Mix together the minced meats, parsley, garlic, hard-boiled eggs, bread and salami. Season to taste with paprika, salt and pepper. Divide the mixture between the cabbage leaves, roll them up and seal them closed with two cocktail sticks.

Heat the vegetable or sunflower oil or butter in a wide pan and fry the onion until well browned. Remove and discard the onion and place the *rambasici* in the pan in a single layer. Cover with half the stock, reduce to a gentle simmer and cook for about 15 minutes, then add the remaining stock, return to a simmer and cook for a further 15 minutes.

Fry the breadcrumbs and Parmesan together in the olive oil in a separate pan until crisp. Arrange the *rambasici* on a warmed serving platter, remove the cocktail sticks, sprinkle with the breadcrumbs and Parmesan and serve at once.

Venetian Boned Stuffed Duck
Anatra col Pien

Served in this region on special occasions, this is a lovely old recipe. The amaretti in the stuffing make it taste particularly unusual and really delicious. An alternative to serving with Salsa Peverada is to choose a side dish of *mostarda di frutta*, crystallized fruits soaked in a mustard syrup: the Italian version of chutney! You can buy it in good delicatessens, especially just before Christmas. Boning a duck is not difficult, but you might like to ask the butcher to do it for you. The greatest benefit to a boned duck is how much easier it is to carve.

SERVES 6

150 g (5 oz) bacon, finely chopped

100 g (4 oz) veal escalope or chicken
   breast, minced

1 duck liver or 2 chicken livers,
   trimmed, washed, dried and chopped

a handful of fresh parsley, chopped

1 stale white bread roll,
   crusts removed, grated

4 amaretti biscuits or 2 macaroons,
   crumbled

5 tablespoons Marsala

1 tablespoon freshly grated Parmesan cheese

salt and freshly milled black pepper

1 egg yolk

1 x 2 kg (4½ lb) oven-ready duck, boned

2 tablespoons olive oil

2 sprigs of fresh rosemary, leaves
   removed and chopped

about 2 wine glasses of dry white or red wine

TO SERVE

Salsa Peverada (see page 128)

4 amaretti biscuits or 2 macaroons, crumbled

Preheat the oven to 180°C/350°F/gas mark 4.

Reserve 25 g (1 oz) of the bacon and mix the remainder with the minced veal or chicken, the duck or chicken livers, parsley and breadcrumbs. Stir the crumbled biscuits into the Marsala until mushy, then add to the meat mixture. Stir in the Parmesan, season to taste with salt and pepper and bind with the egg yolk.

Spoon the mixture into the duck and sew it closed with cook's string. Blend together the olive oil, a little salt, the rosemary and reserved chopped bacon. Put the duck into a lightly oiled roasting tin and spread the rosemary mixture all over it. Roast it in the oven for 1½ hours, basting frequently with the wine and skimming off excess fat. You don't need to use all the wine. Remove the duck from the oven, transfer to a warmed serving platter and carve into thick slices. Crumble the amaretti biscuits or macaroons into the Salsa Peverada and serve with the duck.

Truffle Hunters

As far as I am concerned, Alba, the small town in Piedmont, is the white truffle centre of the universe. Just why the magnificent tuber has chosen this particular corner of the planet to grow so happily and profusely is a mystery to me, but the fact is that it does, and it is one of the best reasons I can think of for visiting the area during the autumn and early winter months.

A whole day at least of a week-long course has to be dedicated to the enjoyment and pursuit of the elusive truffle. After breakfast, the first truffle stop was the annual truffle market, where stalls are set up around the room, all selling truffles, which range in size from small cherry to medium-sized potato. There is also truffle-scented oil for sale, truffle essence and truffle powder. If you want to be a real truffle connoisseur, it is important to acquire a truffle shaver with which to coat your food with literally lashings of truffle slivers as fine as shredded tissue, and if you are going to look for them yourself, you will also need a truffle knife.

As well as the neat displays on the stalls, there are also several men in raincoats and hats who stand around looking shady and wander up to prospective clients muttering the equivalent of, 'Wanna buy a truffle?', which is followed by the production of a crumpled paper bag from the depths of a coat pocket, caked in the pale, dry mud of this area and hiding a cache of tubers.

You will also, if you intend to take up the tricky task of exhuming truffles from the ground, need a dog to help you, as we discovered when we took the students out on a demonstration truffle hunt. It is a cut-throat business, as the truffles are an expensive and much sought-after delicacy which are only available at certain times of the year, so our demonstrators were careful only to let us see the most basic aspects of their skill.

The dog needs to be light in colour so that it stands out, as the best time to seek out the prize so well hidden around the roots of the trees is either at dusk or just before dawn. When the light is bad, the sense of smell is heightened, and so the truffle reveals itself to the dog's snout more easily. The dog is trained for months by being rewarded with bits of truffle to eat. The result is that the dog is actually more keen to eat the truffle than you are! So once he has sniffed one out and starts digging, you need to be right on hand to capture the truffle before the dog swallows it!

We trudged around in the woods, following the dogs and men as they showed us how it is done.

All of a sudden, one of the dogs started yelping and digging at the base of a tree. Everybody ran to the spot, the hunters yelling and waving their arms around. I think they were more surprised than we were! After pulling off the dog, rather more roughly than I thought was necessary, the dog's owner knelt on the ground and scrabbled around a little. He pulled out a tiny little truffle no bigger than my little fingernail. Standing, he announced gravely that this was not a true truffle but a 'signal' truffle, which indicated that this was a site which might in time produce the real thing. It stank of onions and looked like a small, gnarled bulb. But for our students, who had come from the four corners of the globe to experience Piedmont and her cuisine, this was a unique thrill-inducing moment. Some of my students, five years later, still write to me about it! We simply had to go back to the market and buy some now we had witnessed all this!

A few days later, my own precious truffle and I were on an Alitalia flight back to London. The truffle was letting off its earthy, sexy, extremely pungent smell all over the cabin in its own inimitable way. Eventually, one of the stewards asked me if I was carrying one on board. When I said I was, he asked to see it, and once I had opened the jar of rice where it was safely nestling, he took it away to show the pilot and crew, exclaiming with pleasure all the way down the aisle. I got it back, but I ask you, what else could cause such behaviour on a plane?

As I told my students, whatever you use your truffle for, you'll never taste anything so special, so different and so incredibly, deeply redolent of pure animal sex.

Rump Steak in Barolo
Brasato al Barolo

If you cook this properly, keeping the heat so low that the liquid around the meat barely moves, you will end up with meat that is so tender you could cut it with a spoon. If you want to use a cheaper joint than rump, such as silverside, for example, you'll probably find it is even richer in flavour.

SERVES 6

900 g (2 lb) lean rump joint

50 g (2 oz) pork fat, cut into thin strips

2 tablespoons chopped fresh parsley

1 teaspoon chopped fresh sage

½ tablespoon chopped fresh rosemary

2 garlic cloves, finely chopped

salt and freshly milled black pepper

a pinch of freshly grated nutmeg

a pinch of mixed spice

5 tablespoons plain white flour

5 tablespoons olive oil

1 tablespoon unsalted butter

1 onion, sliced

1 carrot, sliced

1 celery stick, sliced

2 dried bay leaves

3–4 small sprigs of fresh parsley

1 bottle of good Barolo

Pierce the join all over with a thick skewer and insert strips of fat wherever possible deep into the meat. Mix together the chopped parsley, sage, rosemary and garlic. Add plenty of salt and pepper, then mix in the spices and about half the flour. Heat the oil and butter together in a large, heavy-based, flameproof casserole dish, add the onion and let it sizzle gently for a few minutes. Meanwhile, roll the meat in the spice mixture, then lay it gently on top of the frying onion. Add the carrot, celery, bay leaves and parsley sprigs. Seal the meat all over, then remove it from the casserole. Drain any excess fat from the casserole. Add the remaining flour and mix it into the other ingredients to make a smooth paste. Pour in about a glass full of Barolo and stir thoroughly. Allow the alcohol to boil off for about 2 minutes, then return the meat to the casserole. Turn it over several times, then pour the remaining Barolo over the joint and cover tightly. Continue to simmer very gently for about 4 hours, turning the joint over occasionally.

When the meat is tender, remove it from the casserole and push the sauce through a food mill or sieve. Taste and adjust the seasoning with salt and pepper if necessary. Slice the meat thickly on to a warmed serving platter, cover with the sauce and serve at once.

Rabbit with Juniper
Coniglio al Ginepro

Many people say that you must soak rabbit joints in milk overnight, or at least for a couple of hours, before rinsing, drying and using to ensure that they are not bitter or stringy. If your rabbit is young enough, you should not need the milk bath, but if in any doubt, go ahead and try it.

SERVES 4

1 young rabbit, jointed

100 g (4 oz) lard or very fatty bacon

1 large onion, finely chopped

1 small bunch of celery leaves, chopped

1 small sprig of fresh rosemary

1 small sprig of fresh sage

1 small sprig of fresh parsley

50 g (2 oz) juniper berries, lightly crushed

2 large ripe tomatoes, peeled,
    seeded and chopped

250 ml (8 fl oz) dry red wine

salt and freshly milled black pepper

250 ml (8 fl oz) meat stock, hot

Wash and dry the rabbit joints thoroughly. Fry the lard or bacon with the onion, celery leaves, herbs and juniper berries. As soon as the onion is soft, add the rabbit joints and brown thoroughly on all sides. Pour over the wine and burn off the alcohol. Stir in the tomatoes. Season, cover and simmer for about 90 minutes, gradually adding the hot stock and basting, until tender.

Pheasant Cooked in Barolo
Fagiano al Barolo

A really amazing way to serve pheasants, especially if finished off with plenty of truffle at the end. Should white truffles prove elusive or just too expensive, you can leave them out altogether or use canned truffles or truffle butter instead. But nothing can really replace the flavour of a fresh, white truffle.

SERVES 6

2 x 2 kg (4½ lb) oven-ready
  pheasants
250 ml (8 fl oz) olive oil
salt and freshly milled black pepper
200 g (7 oz) pancetta, thinly sliced
2 onions, sliced

2 carrots, sliced
2 celery sticks, sliced
2 bottles of youngish Barolo
250 ml (8 fl oz) single cream
white truffle, freshly shaved to taste
TO SERVE
Basic Polenta (see page 123)

Rub the pheasants all over inside and out with a little of the olive oil, salt and pepper, then wrap them carefully in the pancetta. Fry the onion, carrots and celery in the remaining olive oil in a large pan until the vegetables are soft and cooked through. Lay the pheasant on top and seal it all over, then pour over the wine and boil off the alcohol for about 2 minutes. Lower the heat and leave to simmer gently, uncovered, for about 1 hour.

Remove the pheasants from the sauce and joint them carefully. Wrap them in foil and put aside to keep warm. Meanwhile, rub the sauce through a food mill or sieve. Return it to the pan and bring back to boiling point, then take off the heat and stir in the cream. Shave in as much truffle as you can afford and leave the sauce to stand for a moment. Quickly arrange the jointed pheasants on a warmed serving platter and pour over the sauce to smother it completely. Serve at once with slices of polenta.

Veal in Marsala
La Finanziera

This is a rather odd-sounding recipe but is a very old one which crops up frequently in Piedmont and in many guises. This is one of the oldest and most original versions, where the unusual combination of mushroom and gherkin actually works rather well in the end, especially when tempered by the Marsala. You may well come across it with the added ingredient of cream used to bind it all together, which is a much more modern interpretation of this historic dish.

SERVES 6

200 g (7 oz) veal sweetbreads, cleaned

200 g (7 oz) chicken livers, trimmed, washed and dried

4 tablespoons plain white flour

50 g (2 oz) unsalted butter

200 g (7 oz) veal fillet

100 g (4 oz) pickled gherkins in wine vinegar, chopped

100 g (4 oz) fresh porcini mushrooms, sliced

2 dried bay leaves

salt and freshly milled black pepper

2 small glasses of dry Marsala

TO SERVE

toasted bread, Basic Polenta (see page 123), tagliolini or risotto

Gently simmer the sweetbreads in salted water for 30 minutes. Drain and peel, then slice into 1 cm (½ in) thick slices and set aside. Toss the chicken livers in half the flour, then fry them in half the butter in a small pan and set aside.

Cut the fillet into thin slices and toss lightly in the remaining flour. Fry gently in the remaining butter. Add the sweetbreads, chicken livers, gherkins, porcini mushrooms and bay leaves. Season with salt and pepper, mix together, cover and cook gently for about 20 minutes, gradually adding the Marsala as they cook. Serve hot on squares of toasted bread, grilled polenta, freshly cooked and lightly buttered tagliolini or on a bed of plain risotto cooked with a veal or chicken stock.

Chicken Marengo
Pollo alla Marengo

This is apparently the dish which was served to Napoleon and his officers at the end of the famous Battle of Marengo, using only what was left on the cook's cart. This explains, I can only presume, the slightly weird and surreal combination of ingredients!

SERVES 4

1 x 1.25 kg (2½ lb) chicken, jointed

200 ml (7 fl oz) olive oil

4 tablespoons plain white flour

salt and freshly milled black pepper

450 g (1 lb) canned tomatoes,
   seeded and chopped

5 fresh basil leaves, tied together
   with white cotton

400 ml (14 fl oz) dry white wine

1 garlic clove, crushed

200 g (7 oz) mushrooms
   of your choice, sliced

4 large raw prawns (optional), cleaned

4 slices of white bread

4 eggs

a handful of fresh parsley, finely chopped

juice of 1 lemon

Wash the chicken joints and pat them dry with kitchen paper. Heat about 150 ml (4 fl oz) of the olive oil in a wide, deep pan. Dust the chicken with flour and season with salt and pepper. Fry it in the oil for about 15 minutes until brown all over. Add the tomatoes, basil and about 150 ml (5 fl oz) of the wine, then add the crushed garlic, sprinkle with a little salt, stir and cover. Cook for a further 15 minutes. Add the mushrooms, cover again and cook for another 10 minutes.

Meanwhile, pour the remaining wine into a small pan, add 2 pinches of salt and heat to boiling point. Add the prawns, cook for 5 minutes just until pink, then drain and set aside.

Heat the remaining oil in a separate frying pan and fry the bread until crisp and golden. Remove and set aside. Fry the eggs in the same pan.

Scatter the chicken with the parsley, pour over the lemon juice and stir. Remove the chicken from the pan and arrange on a large, warmed serving platter. Surround with the tomato and mushroom sauce, discarding the basil leaves. Arrange the fried bread round the edge, place an egg on each slice of bread, then lay the prawns on top of the eggs. Serve at once with Napoleonic flair.

Trout in the Piedmontese Style
Trota alla Piemontese

I enjoy the combination of the sour vinegar with the sweetness of the sultanas and I have used light balsamic vinegar to good effect in this recipe, although it should be best-quality red wine vinegar according to my Piedmontese purist friends. Try it and see which you prefer.

SERVES 4	**1 x 750 g (1¾ lb) trout, gutted, washed and dried**
50 g (2 oz) sultanas	**2 tablespoons light balsamic vinegar**
1 celery stick, chopped	**or full-flavoured wine vinegar**
1 onion, chopped	**grated zest of 1 lemon**
3–4 leaves of fresh sage	**a pinch of salt**
a sprig of fresh rosemary	**300 ml (10 fl oz) fish stock**
1 garlic clove, chopped	**2 teaspoons plain white flour**
50 ml (2 fl oz) olive oil	**1 tablespoon unsalted butter**

Wash the sultanas and leave them to soak in tepid water until required. Put the celery, onion, herbs, garlic and olive oil into a fish kettle or a pan large enough to take the trout and fry gently for about 5 minutes. Lay the trout in the pan and sprinkle with the balsamic vinegar or wine vinegar and lemon zest. Drain the sultanas and scatter them over the fish. Season with a little salt and pour over the stock. Bring to the boil, cover and simmer gently for about 20 minutes or until the trout is cooked through.

Remove the fish from the pan and place it on a warmed serving platter. Carefully remove the skin and keep the trout hot. Strain the cooking liquid and return it to the heat. Mix together the flour and butter, then whisk the mixture into the hot liquid. Cook thoroughly until thickened and lump free, stirring continuously. Pour this sauce over the fish and serve at once.

The Big Fried Feast
Il Fritto Misto

This feast can be any size you want, depending on how many people are going to eat it with you, and how large the appetites of the diners tend to be. You do not need to cook all the listed ingredients to make a traditional *fricia*, the dialect name for this dish, although some of them must be included for the sake of authenticity. There are no fixed rules in this most typical and traditional Piedmontese dish. The idea is to harmonize the ingredients, flavours and textures according to the season, the mood and personal preferences.

MEATS

veal sweetbreads

veal brains

strips of veal fillet

pork and calves' liver,
  trimmed, washed and dried

smallest lamb cutlets

cockscombs and chicken
  croquettes

Luganega sausage

VEGETABLES

thin slices of aubergine

thin slices of courgette

courgette flowers

thick slices of tomato

sprigs of fresh basil

sprigs of fresh sage

potato croquettes

artichoke segments

MISCELLANEOUS

slices of cheese

apple rings

sweet semolina rings

frogs' legs

amaretti biscuits,
  soaked in milk then
  squeezed dry

mushrooms

slices of pear

GENERAL INGREDIENTS

plain white flour

eggs, beaten

fresh breadcrumbs

salt

olive oil or sunflower oil
  and unsalted butter

Clean and prepare all the meat, vegetables and other ingredients, then cut them into small sections. Toss them in flour, then in beaten egg, and then coat in the breadcrumbs. Some ingredients, such as the artichoke segments, apples, mushrooms and pears are usually cooked in a light batter. Some cooks prefer to coat all the ingredients in batter before frying.

All the ingredients are then fried in generous quantities of olive or sunflower oil mixed with butter. For a lighter dish, fry only in sunflower oil or a similar seed oil. The skill lies in making sure everything is ready simultaneously, bearing in mind that things take different lengths of time to cook. A perfect *fritto misto* is one where all the food reaches the table in batches, but always cooked through and crisp, piping hot and drained of excess grease.

Flat Italian Herb Omelette
Frittata alle Erbe

A *frittata* is an Italian omelette, which is flat and can be very thick or quite thin, depending on personal preference. In Piedmont, for this particular recipe, they use a locally loved herb called *erba balsamica* or *erba della madonna*. I think a mixture of parsley, flatleaf of course, chervil, basil and a little bit of tarragon make a good mixture. What you need to make sure of is that there are enough herbs in the egg mixture for there to be some real substance to the finished *frittata*. In Tuscany, among other things, they make *frittata* with onions, Swiss chard and freshly grated Parmesan.

SERVES 4

a large handful of fresh
    mixed herbs

6 eggs, beaten

4 tablespoons single cream

salt and freshly milled black pepper

40 g (1½ oz) unsalted butter

3 tablespoons olive oil

Remove all the leaves from the herbs, then wash, dry and chop them finely. Place in a bowl with the beaten eggs. Whisk in the single cream and season with salt and pepper. Heat the butter and olive oil in a frying pan until sizzling. Pour in the egg mixture and allow to set and brown on one side. Slide the *frittata* on to a large lid or plate, then invert it back into the pan and fry until brown on the other side. Serve hot or cold.

Garfagnana Night Off

The area of Tuscany to which I belong is called Lunigiana, after the ancient Etruscan city of Luni. It is a small corner of this rich and beautiful region, less well known than the areas around Florence, Siena and Lucca. The area stretching inland from Lunigiana is called Garfagnana. This densely wooded, green and mountainous area is even less well known than Lunigiana.

On one of my very rare evenings off, I borrowed my assistant Euni's battered old car and took myself off up the mountains to visit some old friends. They live in a stunningly beautiful medieval town called Castiglione di Garfagnana. The little town has an almost intact surrounding wall and the solid stone-built towers which provided both look-outs and protection against the enemy during ancient times are as proud and strong now as they were then.

In times long gone, back in the thirteenth century and beyond, this town belonged to the dukes of Lucca. It was for them a vital stronghold, as its northern location made it an important defence position against the d'Estense family of Modena, a hundred kilometres to the north. You can walk right up and inside the main tower, where there is now a house built on the sight of the fortress. I envy the owners of this house as they really do live with a fascinating piece of history. Under their home, they have a tunnel that leads down to the road level, which was once used by the soldiers to bring horses bearing supplies and weapons up to the battle area. From the battlements, you can look out over the red rooftops down to the lovely eleventh-century Basilica of San Michele and the Apuan Alps further away towards the sea. Behind, across the rolling, wooded valley, the ground rises up towards the higher peaks of the Apennines and eventually becomes Emilia Romagna. It is breathtaking, and I took my time drinking it all in as the sun sank down over the Apuan Alps and dusk crept gently over the landscape.

Before it became too dark to find my way back down the curving cobblestone passage, I went back to Vittorio and Adriana's house for dinner. Being mushroom season, and this being one of the best places to find them, Adriana had made a delicious dinner for me. We began with a creamy porcini soup, followed by *Arista di Maiale* (see page 104) with various vegetable, potato and porcini dishes, a refreshing radicchio salad, some delicious local cheeses, and a perfect apple tart.

After dinner, Vittorio and I sat beside the crackling fire with a glass of grappa and I asked him to tell me about the vital importance of the chestnut in this area. Vittorio, who is a passionate homespun expert of his land, its history and customs, explained to me that the chestnut, in its heyday, was not only a basic foodstuff for many people in these mountain communities, especially when times were really hard, but also a commercial commodity.

Chestnuts picked in these woods would be taken down to the coast and bartered for salt. The salt would then be carried all the way up and over the mountains to Emilia Romagna, where it would be sold or bartered for cured meats. Vittorio then began to reminisce about his memories of life here in Castiglione during the war, when a thick gruel made of peeled chestnuts boiled in water, stock or milk would be livened up with the addition of a few freshly gathered mushrooms, a little cheese, or a tiny amount of precious meat.

I was reminded once again of how recently this country has known real hardship, how bitter life must have been for people living a simple existence in the fields, mountains and hillsides. It inspires a terrific humility in me when I hear these stories. I have a sense of great honour and pride to think about how some of the dishes I now teach have actually evolved out of a situation of necessity and grim times.

The roots of some of the recipes are far removed from the trendy restaurants in London, Sydney or Hong Kong. Without knowing whence they came, it is impossible really to make anybody understand what the spirit of this amazingly resilient country is all about. The fact that these dishes are so popular and so widely known is a testament to Italian flair and to *l'arte d'arrangiarsi*, the uniquely Italian ability to cope with having very little and making the very best of it, and to the people who created the original recipes for those dishes, sometimes out of necessity.

Tuscan Pot Roast
Stracotto alla Toscana

By the time this pot roast has finished gently simmering, you should almost be able to slice through it with a spoon. It tastes wonderful served with mashed potatoes and a fresh green vegetable. If you cannot get the heat low enough on top of your hob to simmer so that the liquid around the meat barely moves, then put it into a very low oven.

SERVES 4

1.5 kg (3 lb) beef braising joint (brisket) in a single piece

2–3 garlic cloves, cut into long strips

50 g (2 oz) fatty streaky bacon or pancetta, chopped

1 onion, chopped

1 carrot, chopped

1 celery stick, chopped

75 g (3 oz) unsalted butter

1 litre (1¾ pints) beef stock, kept simmering

salt and freshly milled black pepper

1 tablespoon tomato purée

Pierce the meat all over with the point of a sharp knife and insert the strips of garlic into the meat, adjusting the amount according to how much you like garlic! Place the bacon or pancetta, onion, carrot, celery and butter in a large flameproof casserole and fry for about 8 minutes, stirring constantly. Add the meat and seal it on all sides. Pour over about one-third of the stock, season with salt and pepper and stir in the tomato purée. Bring to the boil, cover and simmer on a very, very low heat for about 6 hours, adding more stock occasionally to prevent the dish from drying out.

When the meat is tender and cooked through, remove it from the casserole and keep it warm. Rub the vegetables and stock left in the casserole through a sieve and adjust the seasoning. Slice the meat thickly and arrange it on a warmed serving platter. Pour over the sieved sauce and serve at once.

Chicken with Rosemary
Pollo alla Diavola

A chicken dish which is simplicity itself to prepare and incredibly delicious to eat, the best way to enjoy it is by cooking the chicken over an open fire. Don't worry about how black the chicken goes on the outside, it is the juicy meat on the inside which counts. Use free-range or corn-fed chicken for the best flavour and texture.

SERVES 6–8

2 x 700 g (1 ½ lb) oven-ready chickens

6 tablespoons olive oil

salt and freshly milled black pepper

4 tablespoons coarsely chopped fresh rosemary leaves

Open up the chickens along the breast bone to open them out and flatten them as much as possible. You can ask your butcher to do this for you but it really is very simple and satisfying to do. Heat the grill or light the barbecue. Press the open chickens hard downwards and outwards to make them as flat as possible. Rub them all over with olive oil, salt and pepper, then sprinkle with the rosemary leaves. Grill on both sides until completely cooked through. The cooking time will vary depending on the heat, but should be about 25 minutes. You should end up with very well-browned, in fact blackened, exteriors and well-cooked but juicy middles. Joint the chickens and serve at once.

Florentine Roast Pork with Rosemary
Arista di Maiale alla Fiorentina

This dish has Renaissance origins. It was specially created for the Ecumenical Council in Florence, the year that the Greek Orthodox Church was invited for the first time. In those days of slow travel, nobody was quite sure how long it might take visitors to arrive, so they had to make a dish which would 'hold' over several days before becoming completely rotten. The natural preservative qualities of rosemary, pepper and garlic, mixed with plenty of salt, would not only have helped to keep the meat fresh but also made sure it smelled great! When the Greeks arrived, they pronounced the dish '*aristos*', which means excellent, and so the name of the dish has stuck through more than half a century. It is the kind of roast which works best with larger joins of meat rather than smaller, as the meat tends to dry out if you use smaller joints. The bigger the piece of meat you start with, the more moist and juicy it will be at the end.

SERVES 6

2 tablespoons fresh rosemary leaves or 1 tablespoon dried rosemary leaves, chopped

2 garlic cloves, finely chopped

salt and freshly milled black pepper

1.5 kg (3 lb) pork loin, boned

2–3 tablespoons olive oil

Preheat the oven to 160°C/325°F/gas mark 3.

Mix together the rosemary and garlic and season with salt and plenty of freshly milled black pepper. Take a skewer and make lots of deep holes in the joint of meat. Rub the rosemary mixture all over the meat, pushing it deep inside the flesh. Tie the joint securely and rub it all over with olive oil, then season the outside with salt and pepper. Roast in the oven for about 2 hours, basting frequently. Turn the joint over each time you baste, until the meat is cooked through and tender. The joint is often allowed to cool and served cold, but you can eat it hot if you wish.

Italian Sausage and Beans
Salsicce e Fagioli

A most satisfying dish in which all the juicy flavours of the sausages permeate through the beans. It only really works with coarse-ground, peppery sausages like they make it Italy but these are now readily available in major supermarkets. For a strong, punchy flavour, use some wild boar sausages.

SERVES 6

500 g (1 lb 2 oz) fresh or
  dried borlotti beans, soaked
  overnight in cold water
2 garlic cloves, chopped
1 onion, chopped
1 celery stick, chopped

1 carrot, chopped
2 teaspoons chopped fresh parsley
2 tablespoons olive oil
1 tablespoon tomato purée
4 tablespoons warm water
12 Italian sausages
salt and freshly milled black pepper

Rinse the beans and then cover them with fresh water. Return to the boil and boil rapidly for 5 minutes. Drain and rinse, then return to the pan, cover generously with fresh water and simmer gently until tender, about 20–30 minutes for fresh or 45–50 minutes for dried.

Meanwhile, fry the garlic, onion, celery, carrot and parsley with the olive oil until all the vegetables are soft. Dilute the tomato purée with the water, then stir it into the pan and add the sausages. Fry together for a few minutes, then add the beans and all their liquid and season with salt and pepper. Bring to the boil, cover and simmer for about 30 minutes until thickened and rich, like a stew, stirring occasionally. Serve warm.

Vegetable and Bean Stew
La Ribollita

The first time I came across this great Tuscan classic was with my dear friend Alvaro Maccioni when we were filming a piece for my BBC television series. In my area of Tuscany, we have a similar dish with a different name, but in the Florence/Pistoia area, where Alvaro comes from, this is the dish and Ribollita is its name. Since my initiation, I have come across many other recipes for the same dish. One of them involves laying thinly sliced onions thickly all over the surface of the soup, drizzling with olive oil and then baking in the oven until golden. You can do that to this recipe if you like!

SERVES 4–6

250 g (9 oz) stale country-style white
  or brown bread, the staler the better

salt and freshly milled black pepper

2 tablespoons olive oil,
  plus extra to serve

3 carrots, coarsely chopped

2 medium-sized potatoes,
  peeled and cubed

2 garlic cloves, finely chopped

2 onions, thinly sliced

1 small cabbage, shredded

any other leaf vegetables of your choice

4 Italian sausages

about 1.2 litres (2 pints) cold water

150 g (5 oz) cooked or canned cannellini beans

TO SERVE

freshly grated Parmesan cheese (optional)

Slice the stale bread and season it with salt and pepper. Brush it thoroughly on both sides with the olive oil. Use it to line a soup tureen or large bowl. Put the vegetables and sausages into a large pan, cover with cold water and season with salt and pepper. Bring to the boil, cover and simmer for about 1½ hours, stirring occasionally and adding more water if required.

Remove the sausages and keep them warm. Stir the beans into the soup and simmer for a further 10 minutes. Adjust the seasoning and pour the soup over the bread in the tureen or bowl. Arrange the sausages on top, then cover and leave to rest for about 10 minutes before serving. Offer a small jug of olive oil so that people can drizzle it over their individual portions as they want to. You can also offer freshly grated Parmesan.

Poultry and Game Stew
Scottiglia

You can just imagine this dish being served to the hungry hunters as they returned from a good day in the hills of Arezzo! Like many Tuscan soups and stews, in this dish the bread is laid at the bottom of the dish to soak up all the juices, flavours and moisture from the stewing meat. Often the bread is the best part of the whole thing!

SERVES 6

1 kg (2¼ lb) mixed jointed meat such as guinea fowl, pork, rabbit, chicken, pheasant and/or pigeon

1 onion, chopped

2 garlic cloves, chopped

a large handful of fresh parsley, chopped

a handful of fresh basil, chopped

100 ml (4 fl oz) olive oil

1 large glass of dry red or white wine

500 g (1 lb 2 oz) fresh ripe, tomatoes, peeled and coarsely chopped

OR 500 g (1 lb 2 oz) passata

salt and freshly milled black pepper

400 ml (14 fl oz) beef or game stock, kept simmering

6 thick slices of coarse, crusty Italian bread

1 large garlic clove

Wash and dry all the meat carefully. Fry the onion, garlic, parsley, basil and olive oil until the onion is soft. Add all the jointed meat and seal on all sides. Pour over the wine, evaporate for 1–2 minutes, then lower the heat. Rub the tomatoes through a sieve to create a purée, then add the purée, or passata if using, to the stewing meat. Season with salt and pepper, cover and simmer very gently for about 2 hours, adding stock occasionally to keep the stew moist and stirring from time to time.

When the meat is all very tender, toast the bread and rub with the garlic clove on both sides. Lay the bread at the bottom of a warmed serving bowl. Pour the stew on top of the bread and serve at once.

Cuttlefish or Squid with Swiss Chard
Totani all'Inzimino

An unusual way of serving cuttlefish or squid, this is absolutely delicious, especially with a slice or two of grilled polenta. A great favourite on the menu at La Famiglia, my friend Alvaro's restaurant in Chelsea. If you can't get chard (although it is very widely available these days) you could use spinach with big, strong leaves.

SERVES 4

150 ml (5 fl oz) olive oil

½ wine glass of dry white wine

300 g (11 oz) passata

500 g (1 lb 2 oz) baby cuttlefish or squid,
  cleaned and sliced (see page 79)

a pinch of salt

1 kg (2¼ lb) Swiss chard

2–3 garlic cloves

1 dried red chilli pepper

2 tablespoons chopped fresh parsley

Pour half the olive oil and all the wine into a large pan, then add the passata and squid. Cook over a gentle heat for about 20 minutes, stirring frequently, until the squid is tender. Season with salt.

Meanwhile, boil or steam the chard until wilted, then drain and squeeze between your hands to remove as much water as possible. Chop coarsely.

Heat the remaining olive oil with the garlic and chilli. Add the chard and the fish. Toss everything together thoroughly over a low heat for about 10 minutes, stirring constantly. Remove the garlic and chilli. Transfer the fish and vegetables to a warmed serving dish, sprinkle with the parsley and serve at once or leave to cool and serve cold.

Rabbit with Olives
Coniglio con le Olive

I didn't realize until very recently, when I was teaching a course in Tuscany and we went shopping for this recipe, that the locals actually have a specific kind of olive which is reserved especially for this dish! It is fine to use any kind of tasty, good-quality black olive, but if you are in the Garfagnana or Lunigiana areas of Tuscany, you can ask for *'olive per fare il coniglio'* and they'll point you towards some very small, black, insignificant-looking little things which taste superb once turned into this dish.

SERVES 6

1 x 2 kg (4½ lb) rabbit, jointed

1 onion, sliced

salt

5 tablespoons olive oil

3 garlic cloves, chopped

2 tablespoons chopped fresh rosemary leaves

3 tablespoons cognac

200 g (7 oz) stoned black or green olives, or a mixture

500 g (1 lb 2 oz) fresh, ripe tomatoes, peeled, seeded and coarsely chopped

250 ml (8 fl oz) chicken stock (optional)

Wash the rabbit joints, dry them carefully and place them in a pan with the onion. Cover thoroughly with salt and place over a lively heat. Allow the rabbit to exude all its liquid, then remove from the heat. Pour away the liquid, rinse the joints carefully and discard the onion. Add the olive oil, garlic and rosemary to the pan and fry for a few minutes, then add the rabbit joints and seal thoroughly all over. Add the cognac and allow the fumes to evaporate. Add the olives and the tomatoes, stir together and cover. Simmer for about 35 minutes, stirring occasionally, or until the rabbit is tender. Add the stock only if the pan appears to be drying out. Serve hot.

Artichoke Feast

Sicily in spring has to be one of the loveliest places to be. The soft, pale sunshine is comfortably warm and the whole island is verdant and luscious, as it has not yet been burned to the crisp, dusty landscape which is inevitable as summer follows on. The olive groves almost sparkle in the light as the sun's rays warm the gnarled trunks and the new growth of silvery leaves nods gently in the breeze. Even the vineyards have a lovely, translucent quality about them, with fresh green leaves unfurling and curly tendrils waving.

One year we were running a course on the island during Easter time. Our hosts invited us to an open-air feast at their old olive mill on Easter Monday, which is traditionally the day on which Italians everywhere go out to eat, either for a picnic or to a restaurant. *Pasquetta*, as this day is called, is for some obscure reason celebrated preferably in the open air, with family and many friends – the more the merrier.

We drove through the olive groves along the dusty track until we came to the old mill house. This was a beautiful, old stone building just waiting to be restored to its former glory and with many of the original features, such as the huge, round millstones for pressing the olives, still intact.

Walking into the courtyard, we were greeted by the sight of trestle tables laid with plates, glasses, cutlery, wine and bread, whilst a huge fire of olive wood burned on the ground in the centre. Standing around in small groups were about 30 people of varying ages. Friends and family had gathered for the feast wearing their best outdoor clothes and with not a hair out of place. I couldn't help thinking how different a similar gathering might have been back at home in England. Unquestionably, there would have been much less of a tangible fashion statement! In any event, everyone was very friendly and obviously very taken with the idea of such a mixing and matching of cultures and backgrounds, even though not everyone was able to communicate in the same language.

The bill of fare consisted of different kinds of *frittata*, cheeses, breads, cured meats and so on, but the fire was being used to create the centrepiece for our meal. I have never seen anything like it before or since. Thrust deep into the embers of the perfectly controlled fire were several dozen artichokes on the end of their long, thick, leafy stalks. The stalks were left outside the heat so that the artichokes could be

manoeuvred easily. What was happening to the artichokes was that they were being burned to a crisp, black crust on the outside, but as soon as they were considered to be cooked in the inside, they would be pulled out and placed on one of the tables.

At this point, using a very sharp knife, the stalks, leaves and all the blackened bits were cut away, revealing the interior of the artichokes to be soft, juicy and perfectly cooked. A little careful removal of the chokes, a dash of olive oil, a squeeze of lemon juice and a little salt resulted in one of the most sublime and memorable flavour sensations I have ever had. Words cannot describe how delicious those artichokes tasted on that fine, warm day. All afternoon, more and more artichokes were carried over to the fire in great bunches, the embers were arranged to form a deep, searing hollow of heat, and the roasting began again. I can't tell you how long they took to cook or how many we ended up eating, but by the time we returned home, our fingers were blackened and our senses deeply satisfied.

It is after this sort of experience, which is so unique and so special, when you feel you have done much more than just eat some food. This is getting to know a country and its customs through your tastebuds, through those most unequivocally honest and evocative senses of smell and taste.

Stuffed Veal Roll
Falsomagro al Sugo

This is one of those great big, important Sicilian dishes which take a long time to prepare but look and taste so wonderful in the end that it makes all the effort worthwhile! The difficulty here is in getting the right piece of meat – whether it be beef or veal – but the size and shape are important so that you can mould the roll. As with all long, slow stewing processes, remember to keep the heat at the lowest ebb so that the liquid around the meat barely moves. That way you will prevent the meat from becoming tough. If Provola or Provolone cannot be found, use a strong-flavoured, peppery cheese which slices well.

SERVES 6

700 g (1½ lb) boneless veal in one large, thick slice

300 g (11 oz) minced veal

75 g (2½ oz) fresh breadcrumbs

75 g (3 oz) Caciocavallo or Parmesan cheese,
  freshly grated

2 hard-boiled eggs, shelled and chopped

1 egg

freshly grated nutmeg or ground cinnamon

salt and freshly milled pepper

50 g (2 oz) Provola or Provolone cheese, sliced

50 g (2 oz) mortadella or salami

4–6 tablespoons olive oil

1 onion, chopped

1 carrot, chopped

1 celery stick, chopped

400 g (14 oz) canned tomatoes,
  drained and chopped

3 tablespoons tomato purée

1 clove

150 ml (5 fl oz) dry red wine

Using a meat mallet, flatten the slice of veal as much as possible to make one large, very thin sheet. If necessary use more than one slice and overlap them as you use the mallet to create a similar effect. Place the sheet of meat on a damp cloth or tea towel.

Mix the minced veal thoroughly with the breadcrumbs and Caciocavallo or Parmesan. Add the chopped hard-boiled eggs and the raw egg to bind the stuffing together. Season with a little nutmeg or cinnamon and salt and pepper. Spread the stuffing over the meat, leaving a border around the edges. Cover the stuffing with the slices of Provola or Provolone and then with the slices of mortadella or salami. Roll up the meat lengthways like a Swiss roll, using the damp cloth or tea towel to help and drawing the ends together very tightly in order to squeeze the roll closed. Remove the cloth and tie the roll securely with kitchen string.

Heat the olive oil in a pan just wide enough to hold the meat, and fry the onion, carrot and celery until the onion is soft and translucent. Moisten with a little water every now and again, or with the juice from the canned tomatoes. Stir in the tomato purée and cook for about 10 minutes, then add the tomatoes and the clove. Season with nutmeg or cinnamon, salt and pepper and simmer gently for about 15 minutes. Lay the meat roll in the pan and baste with the sauce. Pour in the wine and allow the fumes to evaporate, then add enough water almost to cover the meat. Cover the pan and simmer very gently for about 1½ hours. Check the pan occasionally and if necessary add more water to the meat as it simmers.

To serve, remove the meat roll from the pan and take off the string. Slice the meat thinly and arrange it on a warmed serving platter. Boil the sauce in the pan over a lively heat until it has reduced by about half, then pour it all over the sliced meat. Serve hot or cold.

Tuna Steaks with Olive Sauce
Tonno alla Stemperata

Fresh tuna isn't my favourite thing, but when prepared with this lovely sweet-and-sour sauce, it somehow becomes much more interesting. As with all fish dishes, the fresher the fish, the better the whole thing will taste, so make sure you shop with care; it is the first and most important step towards making the dish!

SERVES 6

6 x 150 g (5 oz) tuna steaks

4 garlic cloves, minced

4 celery sticks, chopped

2 tablespoons olive oil

4 tablespoons stoned green olives

4 tablespoons sultanas, soaked in hot water
    for about 12 minutes, then drained

2 tablespoons salted capers, rinsed

3 tablespoons white wine vinegar

salt and freshly milled black pepper

1 heaped tablespoon finely chopped fresh mint

Grill the tuna over a barbecue or under a medium grill until brown and cooked.

Meanwhile, fry the garlic and celery gently in the olive oil until golden brown. Add the olives, drained sultanas and capers and cook over a low heat for 2–3 minutes. Add the wine vinegar and cook over a high heat for 2–3 minutes to evaporate the fumes. Season with salt and pepper, add the mint and stir. Arrange the tuna on a warmed serving platter, pour over the sauce and serve at once.

Sicilian Spring Vegetable Casserole
Fritteda

In the spring, Sicilian cooks make the most of the early crops and turn them into delicious dishes such as this one. Tiny peas, tender broad beans and the first, small, soft artichokes are cooked together so that all their flavours blend, and then sprinkled with a dash of best-quality wine vinegar at the very end. This last ingredient, together with the fact that the dish is served cold, makes *fritedda* into a kind of cooked salad. As artichokes show signs of oxidizing after they have been cut and prepared, drop them into a basin of cold water and lemon juice to prevent them from going brown and ugly. Drain and dry them carefully before proceeding with the recipe.

SERVES 6

12 small, tender artichokes

5–6 spring onions, sliced

3 tablespoons water

4 tablespoons olive oil

salt and freshly milled black pepper

900 g (2 lb) very young broad beans, shelled

900 g (2 lb) very young peas, shelled

2 tablespoons white wine vinegar

Slice off the tips of the artichokes, remove all the tough outer leaves and peel the bases. Be merciless, however extravagant it may seem, for one tough artichoke leaf can ruin an otherwise perfect mouthful. Cut the artichokes into quarters. Remove the choke, if it has formed, together with any prickly tips of the inner leaves, then cut each quarter in three to create very fine wedges.

Place the spring onions and water in a heavy-based pan and cook over a medium heat, stirring constantly, until the water evaporates. Add the olive oil and sauté the spring onions for a few minutes until pale golden. Add the artichokes, moisten with a little more hot water and add salt to taste. Cover and cook over a low heat for 5 minutes. Add the broad beans and a little more hot water. Cover and cook for a further 5 minutes. Add the peas, cover and cook for 5 minutes more, then sprinkle with the wine vinegar and some pepper. Correct the salt and cook over a medium-high heat, uncovered, for 2–3 minutes until the wine vinegar has evaporated. Leave to cool, then chill for 24 hours and serve cold.

Simple Fish Casserole
Zuppetta di Pesce

This is the easiest recipe for making a really Italian-tasting fish casserole. The bread soaks up all the flavours and juices of the fish and is eaten at the end, once all the fish has been enjoyed. Please make sure that the mussels are really fresh and properly cleaned.

SERVES 6

1.5 kg (3 lb) filleted white fish such as cod, monkfish, haddock, plaice

1 kg (1¾ lb) fresh, live mussels in their shells

8 tablespoons olive oil

4 garlic cloves, finely chopped

4 tablespoons chopped fresh parsley

salt and freshly milled black pepper

200 ml (7 fl oz) fish stock

1 large glass of dry white wine

12 thin slices of ciabatta bread, toasted

1 garlic clove

TO SERVE

2–3 tablespoons chopped fresh flatleaf parsley

grated zest of ½ lemon

Prepare all the fish first. Trim it carefully, then wash and pat it dry. Scrub the mussels thoroughly and scrape off any barnacles, removing the little beard at the side. Soak for 30 minutes or so each time in two or three changes of fresh, clean water, rinsing thoroughly between each soak.

Heat the olive oil in a deep pan with the garlic and parsley for about 5 minutes. Add the fish and stir. Season with salt and pepper and pour over the fish stock. Add the mussels. Pour over the wine and allow to boil quickly for about 1 minute to evaporate the alcohol. Cover tightly and simmer very gently for about 15 minutes. Rub the toasted bread with the garlic and use the bread to line a large, wide bowl. Discard any mussels which have not opened and do not attempt to force them open – just throw them away. Pour the hot fish casserole all over the bread and serve at once, sprinkled with a little flatleaf parsley and grated lemon zest.

Swordfish Steaks with Olive and Parmesan Stuffing
Involtini di Pesce Spada

A bit fiddly, but delicious, unless the fish slices are very large and easy to manoeuvre on to the skewers, it is better to tuck everything into a baking dish and pop it all in a hot oven to cook, as things will look much neater.

SERVES 6

1.25 kg (2¾ lb) round swordfish steak

I large red onion

12–15 bay leaves

2 tablespoons olive oil

100 g (4 oz) dried breadcrumbs

FOR FILLING I

5 tablespoons chopped fresh parsley

5 garlic cloves

3 tablespoons currants, soaked in hot
   water for 5 minutes, then drained

3 tablespoons pine kernels

salt and freshly milled black pepper

1–2 tablespoons olive oil

FOR FILLING 2

4 tablespoons stoned green olives

3 tablespoons salted capers, rinsed

2 tablespoons chopped fresh parsley

3 tablespoons dried breadcrumbs

4 tablespoons freshly grated Caciocavallo,
   Parmesan or Pecorino cheese

2–3 tablespoons olive oil

To make the first filling, finely chop the parsley and garlic. Add the currants and pine kernels and chop roughly. Season, then stir in the olive oil, mixing well.

To make the second filling, chop the olives, capers and parsley together until fine. Stir in the breadcrumbs and cheese, and blend with the olive oil.

Bone and skin the fish, cut it into quarters, then slice each quarter across into six thin slices, roughly 7.5 x 10 cm (3 x 4 in) and less than 5 mm (⅛ in) thick. Irregularity won't show in the end! Peel the onion, cut it into quarters or sixths, then separate it into pieces that are wide enough to thread on a skewer.

Place a teaspoon of the filling of your choice on one end of each slice of fish and roll them up neatly. Thread a piece of onion on to a skewer, then add a fish roll, a bay leaf, another roll of fish, then a slice of onion, and so on. Continue until you have six skewers. Run a second skewer through, parallel to the first and about 2.5 cm (1 in) distant, to hold the fish rolls steady. Moisten with oil and then dip lightly in the breadcrumbs. Grill gently, over barbecue coals or under a grill, for 8–10 minutes until cooked through and golden, turning occasionally, or bake in a preheated oven at 200°C/400°F/gas mark 6 for about 20 minutes.

4

Side
Dishes
and
Sauces

This is a motley collection of various recipes which could not be fitted into any other category. You'll find vegetable dishes, curiosities and sauces gathered here, as they form part of each region's tapestry of dishes and therefore belong in the courses I teach.

Vegetables in particular are often treated with great reverence in Italy and are turned into much more than just an accompanying vegetable; they become dishes in their own right. Alternatively, they can be cooked as simply as possible and perhaps just dressed with olive oil and lemon juice, or quickly tossed in a hot frying pan with a little olive oil and a crushed garlic clove. It is rare indeed that vegetables in Italy are served 'naked' unless they are either considered so spectacularly fresh or special that they need nothing added to them – or else the cook is on a diet.

The most important accompaniment to any Italian meal is good bread. This is vital for mopping up your plate and for cleansing your mouth so that it is ready to appreciate the flavours of the various dishes. No meal can be truly Italian without some crusty, fresh bread with really good flavour and texture to complement the dishes.

Basic Polenta
Polenta

Polenta is a staple of the northern Italian diet, in particular of the Veneto area. You can buy a quick-cook version, which you mix up in just five minutes, but I personally would recommend you try the traditional version and see what a difference it makes before you decide! With traditional polenta, you need to stir constantly for about 45 minutes, but the end result, in my opinion, is different from the quick-cook variety. Because it is such a long-winded operation, one tends to make a large batch in one go. After serving it freshly cooked (and thus soft) the first time, it can be left to set and can then be sliced up and used fried or grilled over the subsequent days. Many people find polenta hard to take, possibly because it is rather bland, but as such it serves as the perfect foil for highly flavoured dishes or very strong-flavoured cheeses.

SERVES 6

1.75 litres (3 pints) cold water

a pinch of salt

200–250 g (7–8 oz) ground cornmeal (polenta flour)

Pour the water and salt into a wide, heavy-based, preferably copper pan, place it over a high heat and bring to the boil. Trickle the polenta flour into the boiling water in a fine rain with one hand while whisking constantly with the other (this is easier to do with a friend). When all the polenta flour has been whisked into the water, reduce to a medium to low heat, then begin to stir with a strong, long-handled wooden spoon until the polenta comes away from the sides of the pan. This will take 40–50 minutes and requires patience, energy and a strong elbow. Turn the polenta out on to a wooden board and smooth it into a mound shape with spatulas. Leave it to stand for about 5 minutes, then cut it into slabs and serve hot with its accompanying stew, fricassee or casserole, or with a slice of very strong-flavoured cheese such as Gorgonzola. Alternatively, leave it to go completely cold, then slice it like bread and grill, fry or bake it as required.

Stewed Beans
Fagioli in Umido

This dish is best made with fresh beans although you can use dried. If so, you will need to soak them in cold water overnight, then boil fast in fresh water for five minutes before rinsing and continuing with the recipe. I like to serve this alongside some grilled sausages, or with a roast pork or beef dish, or with game.

SERVES 4

1 kg (2¼ lb) fresh borlotti or haricot beans	2–3 fresh sage leaves
	3–4 tablespoons olive oil
	350 g (12 oz) very ripe, soft tomatoes, washed and sieved
3 garlic cloves, crushed	salt and freshly milled black pepper

Shell the beans and cover them in cold water, bring to the boil and simmer for about 20 minutes until tender.

Fry the garlic and sage gently in the olive oil until golden brown. Add the beans, stir together, then add the sieved tomatoes. Simmer gently for 20 minutes. Check and adjust the seasoning just before serving.

Venetian Pan-roasted Potatoes
Patate Arrosto alla Veneziana

It is important to use yellow-fleshed, waxy potatoes and to cook them with their skins on, so scrub them well before you start. If you prefer, you could roast these potatoes in the oven instead of cooking them in a large frying pan.

SERVES 4

550 g (1¼ lb) medium-sized potatoes	3 tablespoons extra virgin olive oil
1 large white onion, sliced	a pinch of salt
40 g (1½ oz) unsalted butter	25 g (1 oz) fresh parsley, chopped

Peel the potatoes and cut them lengthways into eight segments. Fry the onion in the butter and olive oil in a large, deep frying pan until the onion is soft. Add the potatoes and cook for about 20 minutes until tender and crisp, turning frequently. Sprinkle with salt and serve piping hot with a dusting of chopped parsley.

Stewed Venetian Peppers
Peperonata alla Veneziana

This is the Venetian version of a recipe which is made all over Italy. The texture of the finished dish is very soft and squashy, almost like jam. It is essential to keep everything moist during the cooking process and to make sure the peppers are very sweet. Fabulous with either chicken or fish, you can also serve it on its own or as a topping for toasted crostini or bruschetta.

SERVES 4

500 g (1 lb 2 oz) yellow or
   green peppers

400 g (14 oz) aubergines

1 garlic clove

75 g (3 oz) unsalted butter

5 tablespoons extra virgin olive oil

300 g (11 oz) small onions

300 g (11 oz) small tomatoes

½ wine glass of dry white wine

salt

Prepare the peppers and aubergines and cut them into even-sized chunks. Fry the garlic in the butter and olive oil until golden brown, then discard the garlic. Add the onions and cook until just soft, then add the peppers, aubergines and tomatoes. Sprinkle with the wine and add salt to taste. Cover and simmer gently for about 1 hour, taking care to keep the heat low and to stir frequently.

Pan-grilled Radicchio
Radicchio in Padella

If you like slightly bitter flavours, then this is the perfect dish for you. Although radicchio is often seen as a salad vegetable in the UK, in Italy it is used a great deal as a cooked vegetable. There are three main varieties – Verona, Chioggia and Trevisana – and they are all used to make all kinds of dishes, including delicious pasta sauces, risottos, savoury pies, cakes and other delicacies. To make the following recipe, you must start off by using radicchio which has a good root stump.

SERVES 4

2 large heads of radicchio
  with root stump

a little olive oil

salt and freshly milled
  black pepper

Heat a frying pan until piping hot. Cut the radicchio in half lengthways through the root stump. The root stump will hold each half intact. Brush each half with olive oil and season with salt and pepper. Lay the radicchio in the pan and cook for about 20 minutes, turning once, until slightly blackened and soft. Serve hot.

Venetian Sauce for Roast Game
Salsa Peverada

It may seem quite peculiar to blend the flavours of this sauce with the already very intense taste of the game, but it actually works really well. Although the sauce is created specifically for roasted game, it is also fabulous with plain roasted chicken.

SERVES 4

3 salted anchovies, boned, rinsed and finely chopped

4 oz (100 g) chicken livers, trimmed, washed, dried and finely chopped

2 rashers unsmoked back bacon, finely chopped

grated rind of I lemon

I garlic clove

5 tablespoons olive oil

I tablespoon white wine vinegar

salt and freshly milled black pepper

Simmer all the ingredients except the wine vinegar, salt and pepper over a gentle heat for about 15 minutes until soft and cooked through. Stir frequently to achieve as smooth a texture as possible. Discard the garlic. Sprinkle with the white wine vinegar, season with salt and pepper and stir well. Serve very hot.

Winter Pesto Sauce
Pesto d'Inverno

In both Piedmont and Tuscany, both of which border with Liguria to the north and south respectively, a winter pesto is made with walnuts. This replaces the gorgeously green summer pesto made with masses of fresh basil. It is used mostly to dress pasta, although it is also marvellous when used rather like the almond pesto on page 66, as part of a stuffing, or stirred into soups and stews. Try to use very fresh walnuts with plenty of milky juice so that the sauce is very moist. Walnuts in Piedmont are especially fabulous, and there is an old tradition of using walnut oil in this region. All the proportions below depend very much on the quality of the walnuts, so you may need to adjust them slightly as you prepare your own pesto sauce.

MAKES 500 ML (17 FL OZ)

500 g (1 lb 2 oz) shell-on walnuts

5 garlic cloves

100 ml (3½ fl oz) olive oil

50 ml (2 fl oz) walnut oil

freshly grated Parmesan cheese (optional)

salt and freshly milled black pepper

2–3 tablespoons fresh, white breadcrumbs

Carefully crack and shell all the walnuts. If the skins are very tough, the walnuts will have to be peeled. I realize this is a hugely tiresome task, but blanching them in boiling water for a minute will help a little!

Put the walnuts and garlic in a mortar and pound them to a paste. Gradually add the oils, pounding continuously, until you have reached a reasonably smooth texture. Add as much Parmesan as you like, or leave it out if you prefer. Season with salt and pepper to taste and finally blend in the breadcrumbs to give the sauce a little more body. Alternatively, you can use a food processor instead of doing it all by hand.

The Mushroom Hunt

Every year, come the autumn, local Italian papers throughout the country fill several pages with ghastly stories of entire families wiped out by picking and eating the wrong mushrooms. Having been brought up with these stories read aloud to me in the kitchen at home as a way of ensuring that I would never die this hideous death, I always approach the subject of wild mushroom-picking with more than a little nervous concern. So when the idea of taking a group of paying students on a mushroom foray was suggested and then seized upon with vigorous enthusiasm, I felt a definite quiver of anxiety run up my spine.

I spent much of my time in the days leading up to the event reading as many books as I could lay my hands on. I gathered and absorbed information and committed countless images of edible and non-edible species to memory. Though by no means an expert, I felt I could now be trusted a little further than I could have been before.

The day began very early indeed, with picnic preparations for fifteen on the large marble table, while simultaneously dealing with breakfast. Eventually, having made quite sure that everybody was appropriately clothed, we set off for a private estate where we had been granted free access and where nobody else with the same intentions had been before us in the much earlier hours of the morning. After setting down the picnic baskets and handing out mushroom baskets and knives with which to cut the mushrooms without damaging them, we all set off, arranging to meet back at the picnic site in two hours. At first, everybody rather nervously moved around together, but gradually we began to spread out and small groups of two or three seemed to form naturally and wander off under the trees.

I stuck with Martin, who knows a lot about mushrooms, in the hope that I would be able to gain a lot from his expertise. I was amply rewarded because he taught me a great deal, especially about how and where to look depending on what I was looking for. Best of all, we gathered a big basket of mushrooms. It is an intensely rewarding feeling, when you carry away with you a basket of items which you have gathered, caught or otherwise obtained for yourself. It was with much pride that we returned laden and glowing to the picnic site.

We had exhaustively described the edible varieties likely to be sighted, explained the terrain and the trees, and been careful to explain to everybody that they should

never place any specimen they were unsure about in the basket with edible varieties. Those thought to be really dangerous were to be put into jacket pockets away from everything else. We were therefore reasonably confident that nobody would have put themselves at risk. How wrong we were!

A glass of red in hand, I greeted the foragers as they returned to camp in varying states of satisfaction. Some had done very well, with parasols and chanterelles a-plenty. Others had but a handful of obscure findings stuffed in an anorak pocket, mostly too crushed to identify with any accuracy. One person had just a single, perfect, snow-white puffball, as bald and smooth as a newborn baby's head. But it was the last basket that really caused the scene!

When we came to the final selection, Martin let out a yell and stepped back several paces. I think his exact words were something about wiping out the entire population of Liverpool if so much as one of the fungi in the basket were to enter the water system of that fair city! They were to be discarded immediately and anybody who had even slightly touched any of them was to wash their hands very thoroughly with soap and scalding hot water. I am still unsure if he was over-reacting, but we did it anyway, just to be completely safe.

The picnic, as they are often wont to do, rapidly restored everybody's rattled feelings. Martin continued to mutter darkly about the dangers of poisonous mushrooms, sounding for all the world like one of those newspaper articles which have always made me so nervous.

That night at dinner we had course after course based around our mushrooms: polenta with mushrooms, mushroom crostini, risotto and taglioni, mushroom soup and salad, chicken breasts in a mushroom sauce and sea bass with mushrooms, mushroom *frittata*, mushroom pizza and mushroom tart! And all of us were perfectly well – though more than over-stuffed!

Mushrooms with Garlic and Oregano
Funghi a Funghetto

*B*oletus edulis, ceps or porcini – call them what you will, they are the king of the mushroom world! You do need to use fresh ones for this recipe, but if porcini are not around, try the same method with any other type of mushroom, either wild or cultivated.

SERVES 6

4–5 tablespoons olive oil

500 g (1 lb 2 oz) fresh porcini
  mushrooms, thinly sliced

salt and freshly milled
  black pepper

1 large pinch of dried oregano

3–4 garlic cloves, finely chopped

Heat the olive oil in large pan for about 1 minute, then add the mushrooms, stir and season with salt and pepper. Cover and cook for about 15 minutes, stirring occasionally, to allow the mushrooms to cook through completely. Remove from the heat and stir in the oregano and garlic. Cover and leave to stand for 2 minutes, then serve at once.

Assistants and Pumpkins

My friend Greg, who used to be my assistant chef before computers got the better of him, once made Pumpkin-stuffed Baked Onions (see page 136) without me on a course in Piedmont. I had taken the group to a wine-tasting or something, leaving Greg in charge of making dinner. One of the vegetable accompaniments was this dish. I returned about an hour before dinner was due to be served and everything in the kitchen seemed to be fine. We were serving a Fontina and bean soup, Pheasant Cooked in Barolo (see page 93) with mashed potatoes, the aforementioned onions and sautéed chard, followed by tiny Tomini, a local cheese, warmed in the oven and drizzled with hot local honey. The table was set, the table flowers looked wonderful and the wine was ready to be poured. I felt completely relaxed and happy that once again, my complete faith in Greg's ability had not been misguided.

At dinner that night, our hostess, in whose home we were staying, took one mouthful of the onion dish and practically spat it out. I was sitting opposite her and immediately felt a panic begin to flood through me. What was wrong? Quickly, I took a mouthful of onion and plenty of the stuffing. To my horror, it was sour, bitter and inedible! Apologising like mad, I quickly told everyone just to admire the onions, not to eat them. The rest of the dinner was delicious and passed without incident.

By the time the second round of coffee and the third round of grappa had passed, the kitchen was cleared up for the next day and the real late-night crowd were settling into a long game of cards, I had almost forgotten the onions. Wearily, I took my leave and went to my room, trying not to think about whether we had everything we needed for the next day.

Sometime in the very wee hours I woke up with the onions on my mind. What could have gone wrong? Greg is an excellent chef and scrupulously efficient. I could not work it out.

The next morning, at our usual early hour, Greg and I met again in the kitchen where tea, coffee and general breakfast preparations were in full flow. As we cleared breakfast away and began to set out the ingredients and utensils for the lesson, I quizzed him about what he had done. Poor Greg was mortified, and together we pored over the recipe. Eventually, he revealed that he had used the decorative gourds for the filling instead of the pumpkin I had bought for the purpose. The gourds had been arranged above the sink as a cheerful, colourful touch in the kitchen, but they were definitely not edible!

The role of assistant on the courses is a very special one, and over the years I have had the privilege of working with several fantastic people who have gone on to become valued friends. It is never an easy task to be the person who makes every-thing happen behind the scenes, apparently so effortlessly, and who makes my job easier in a hundred different ways – pumpkins aside.

Pumpkin-stuffed Baked Onions
Cipolle Ripiene di Magro

This is a very pretty and unusual dish which I serve alongside roast turkey or duck for big occasions like Christmas dinner. Make sure the onions have a good strong, sweet flavour and that the *mostarda di frutta* (candied fruits in a mustard syrup) have plenty of peppery bite to them for a good contrast of flavours.

SERVES 6

900 ml (1½ pints) water

a pinch of salt

6 very large, even-sized onions

500 g (1 lb 2 oz) pumpkin, peeled, seeded and cut into chunks

125 g (4½ oz) *mostarda di frutta*, finely chopped, plus syrup

1 large egg, beaten

¼ teaspoon freshly grated nutmeg

175 g (6 oz) amaretti biscuits, crushed

50 g (2 oz) unsalted butter

Preheat the oven to 200°C/400°F/gas mark 6.

Pour the water into a large pan with the salt and bring to the boil. Drop in the peeled onions and the pumpkin and boil for about 10 minutes or until the onions are about three-quarters cooked. Take out the onions and place on a perforated tray to drain. Drain the pumpkin very thoroughly, squeeze dry and then put into a bowl. Add the *mostarda di frutta* with its syrup, the egg, nutmeg and amaretti biscuits. Mix all this together very thoroughly.

Push out and discard the central core of the onions. Fill each onion with the pumpkin stuffing and level the top. Use some of the butter to grease an ovenproof dish very thoroughly, then place the onions in the dish and dot each onion with the remaining butter. Bake in the oven for about 40 minutes or until the onions are cooked through. Serve hot or cold.

Swiss Chard with Garlic
Bieta in Padella

A most underrated vegetable, in my opinion, Swiss chard is deliciously simple to cook too! If you can't buy it, try to buy bok choi from the supermarket or a Chinese greengrocer. Baby bok choi will be more tender and taste sweeter.

SERVES 6

3 heads of Swiss chard, shredded

2 garlic cloves, crushed

100 ml (4 fl oz) olive oil

salt and freshly milled
  black pepper

Make sure the chard is all perfectly clean. Heat the garlic and olive oil together in a very wide pan. Add the chard and toss together thoroughly until the chard wilts and softens. Cover the pan to preserve the colour and help the chard to cook. Uncover and stir frequently for about 20 minutes until the card is cooked to your taste. Season generously with salt and pepper and serve at once.

Carrots in Milk
Carote al Latte

Young turnips are also very good cooked this way, especially if you use lemon instead of orange zest at the end.

SERVES 6

750 g (1¾ lb) carrots, thickly
  sliced into rounds

salt and freshly milled
  black pepper

1 heaped tablespoon unsalted butter

150 ml (5 fl oz) full-cream milk

1 egg yolk, beaten

1 heaped tablespoon chopped fresh parsley

1 teaspoon very finely chopped orange zest

Bring a pan of salted water to the boil, toss in the carrots and boil quickly for 5 minutes. Drain the carrots thoroughly, then put them in a large frying pan with the butter and two-thirds of the milk. Season to taste, then cook for a further 6 minutes until tender, stirring occasionally. Whisk the remaining milk and the egg yolk, then pour over the carrots. Heat until the sauce thickens, then transfer to a warmed serving dish. Sprinkle with the parsley and orange zest and serve at once.

Green Beans in the Florentine Style
Fagiolini alla Fiorentina

This is a sure-fire way to liven up the most tasteless of green beans. Even frozen green beans, which rarely taste of anything at all, take on a new lease of life with this very simple recipe.

SERVES 4

500 g (1 lb 2 oz) green beans,
   topped and tailed

1 large onion, thinly sliced

5 tablespoons olive oil

1 heaped tablespoon tomato purée

4 tablespoons hot water

1 teaspoon fennel seeds,
   crushed to a powder

salt and freshly milled black pepper

Boil the beans in lightly salted water until just tender. Meanwhile, fry the onion in the olive oil in a wide frying pan until soft. Dilute the tomato purée in the water, then stir it into the pan with the crushed fennel seeds. Drain the beans very thoroughly, then toss them into the pan. Mix everything together very thoroughly and season to taste with salt and pepper. Cover and cook through for another 5–10 minutes, then serve at once.

Stewed Mushrooms
Funghi in Umido

I really love mushrooms cooked in this way. The tomato purée and lemon juice combine to give a wonderfully sweet-and-sour finish to the dish. Excellent with lots of crusty bread or as a side dish with eggs fried in plenty of butter, it works best if made in a flameproof terracotta pan, but otherwise use a pan which is good and heavy and where the mushrooms fit snugly.

SERVES 4

500 g (1 lb 2 oz) small wild
   or cultivated mushrooms

100 ml (4 fl oz) olive oil

4 garlic cloves, crushed

1 sprig of fresh rosemary

salt and freshly milled black pepper

a little vegetable or chicken stock, kept hot (optional)

1 tablespoon tomato purée

juice of 1 lemon

Clean the mushrooms carefully with a soft cloth and cut them into manageable pieces if they are large. Heat the olive oil with the garlic and rosemary in a large, preferably terracotta pan until the garlic has gone very brown. Discard the garlic and rosemary and add the mushrooms. Stir thoroughly to coat with oil and season to taste with salt and pepper. Continue to cook them gently, adding the stock a spoonful at a time only if they appear to be drying out too quickly. When they are almost cooked, stir in the tomato purée and the lemon juice. Stir again and finish off the cooking, then serve directly from the terracotta pan. The total cooking time will be about 30 minutes.

Florentine-style Spinach
Spinaci alla Fiorentina

To make this into a complete meal, make some shallow hollows in the sauce on top of the spinach and crack into each hollow one or two raw eggs per person. The eggs will bake and set as the dish heats through and the top becomes lightly browned. Serve it with lots of crusty bread. Alternatively, serve as a vegetable side dish with plain, light meat, poultry or fish dishes, or even as a light and appetizing starter.

SERVES 4

I kg (2¼ lb) fresh spinach, thoroughly
   washed and tough stems removed

3 tablespoons olive oil

2 garlic cloves, crushed

salt and freshly milled black pepper

200 ml (7 fl oz) béchamel sauce
   (see page 47)

100 g (4 oz) Parmesan cheese,
   freshly grated

Preheat the oven to 220°C/425°F/gas mark 7.

Rinse the spinach several times in fresh water. Place in a pan with just the water remaining on the leaves and cook until wilted. As soon as it is all soft, drain and cool, then squeeze dry and chop coarsely.

Heat the olive oil with the garlic in a wide frying pan until the garlic is well browned. Discard the garlic and tip the spinach into the oil. Toss thoroughly and heat through. Season to taste with salt and pepper.

Meanwhile, heat the béchamel and stir in three-quarters of the Parmesan. Butter an ovenproof dish thoroughly and tip the spinach into it. Pour over the béchamel, sprinkle with the remaining Parmesan and bake in the oven for about 5 minutes or until the top is lightly browned.

Pan-fried Turnip Tops with Oil and Garlic
Rape Amare in Padella

A traditional way of cooking turnip tops, these are much less common in Britain than in Italy and since they have a very bitter flavour, they are not to everyone's liking. However, this is also a very good way of cooking any kind of cabbage, including the Tuscan cabbage known as *cavolo nero*, or black cabbage, which you can see in supermarkets and greengrocers these days.

SERVES 4	
	75 ml (3 fl oz) olive oil
750 g (1 ½ lb) turnip tops	2–3 garlic cloves, sliced
or cabbage	salt and freshly milled black pepper

Clean and trim the turnip tops or cabbage carefully. Slice the large leaves into smaller sections, discard any hard spines and slice the core neatly. Wash the turnip tops or cabbage repeatedly in several changes of cold water. Drain and dry thoroughly. Bring a large pan of water to the boil, throw in the turnip tops or cabbage and boil for exactly 12 minutes. Drain and rinse thoroughly under cold running water. Squeeze them dry very thoroughly, then chop them very coarsely.

Heat the oil and garlic until the garlic is light golden brown, then add the turnip tops or cabbage. Toss together quickly and season to taste with salt and pepper. Once heated through and well flavoured by the oil and garlic, they are ready to serve.

Ligurian Pesto
Pesto Ligure

I know this is not a Tuscan recipe but my own corner of the region is right on the border with Liguria and therefore pesto was commonplace throughout my life. It is the quintessential symbol of a glorious Ligurian summer day, a sauce with a unique perfume and flavour which should be used throughout the winter (sparingly) to liven up everything from soups to stuffings, pies to potatoes. It tastes especially good brushed over and spooned inside a chicken breast before grilling or roasting.

MAKES ENOUGH TO DRESS
500 G (I LB 2 OZ) PASTA

4 large handfuls of fresh basil
  leaves, washed but not bruised,
  dried carefully

a large pinch of rock salt

2 garlic cloves, halved

a handful of pine kernels

2 tablespoons freshly grated
  Parmesan cheese

about ½ wine glass of best-quality olive oil

salt and freshly milled black pepper

If you use a pestle and mortar, remember to press the basil leaves against the sides, do not bang downwards as usual. Put the basil, salt and garlic into the mortar or food processor and reduce to a smooth green purée. Add the pine kernels and Parmesan and blend these in, then begin to add the oil a little at a time until you have reached a smooth, creamy texture. Season with salt and pepper and use as required.

Braised Peas with Olive Oil
Piselli all'Olio

I adore peas cooked like this and I often serve them alongside meatballs stewed in a simple tomato sauce, or sometimes I use them as a filling for a soft, warm focaccia or in a *frittata*. In fact, they are so delicious, I like them just on their own!

SERVES 4

1.25 kg (2½ lb) fresh
  peas, shelled
OR 450 g (1 lb) shelled
  fresh or frozen peas

1 onion, thinly sliced
100 ml (4 fl oz) olive oil
½ teaspoon caster sugar
salt and freshly milled black pepper

Soak the peas in cold water for about 1 hour. Meanwhile, gently fry the onion in a terracotta or cast iron pan with the olive oil until soft and golden. Drain the peas and add to the onion. Season with sugar, salt and pepper, then cover and simmer until soft and cooked through. The timing will depend upon how large or small the peas are; tiny little ones will only take about 4 minutes, larger, fat peas with tougher skins could take up to 15 minutes. Serve at once.

Aubergine Fritters
Frittelle di Melanzane

Another very versatile dish, you can serve these moist little aubergine balls either hot or cold as an antipasto or to accompany grilled meats or poultry. They have a lovely soft texture and the sultanas give just a hint of sweetness.

SERVES 4–6

1 kg (2¼ lb) aubergines, thickly sliced

salt

90 g (3½ oz) sultanas

2 eggs yolks

75 g (3 oz) Pecorino cheese, freshly grated

a large pinch of dried oregano

¼ teaspoon freshly grated nutmeg

freshly milled black pepper

3 tablespoons plain white flour

1 egg, beaten

3–4 tablespoons fresh white breadcrumbs

oil for deep-frying

Put the sliced aubergines into a pan and cover with cold salted water. Put a heavy plate on top and leave for about 45 minutes. Meanwhile, cover the sultanas with water and let them soak for 45 minutes.

Drain the aubergines and squeeze out as much water as you can by hand. Put them back in the pan with enough fresh water to cover. Bring to the boil, then boil for about 5 minutes. Drain well, chop as finely as possible and place in a bowl.

Drain and dry the sultanas and add to the bowl with the egg yolks, Pecorino, oregano, nutmeg and plenty of black pepper. Mix together, then shape into walnut-sized balls and toss them first in the flour, then the beaten egg, then the breadcrumbs. Heat the oil and fry the fritters for about 10 minutes until crisp and golden. Drain on kitchen paper and serve hot or cold.

Aubergine and Olive Salad
Caponata

This old and traditional Sicilian recipe makes the most of the island's favourite vegetable: the aubergine. To develop the flavours properly, make this dish the day before you eat it. It is lovely as a topping for crostini or bruschetta, or inside warmed focaccia.

SERVES 6

900 g (2 lb) aubergines, cubed

1 tablespoon salt

100 ml (3½ fl oz) olive oil

40 g (1½ oz) onion, chopped

250 g (9 oz) assorted pickles such
   as onions, peppers and gherkins

25 g (1 oz) salted capers, rinsed

6 celery leaves, chopped

50 g (2 oz) green olives, stoned

1 tablespoon granulated sugar

1 wine glass of red wine vinegar

2 tablespoons pine kernels

Cover the cubed aubergines with salt, put them in a colander in the sink and leave them to drain out their bitter juices for about 1 hour or longer if possible. Wash and dry them thoroughly.

Divide the olive oil between two deep pans. Fry the aubergine cubes in one pan until soft and well coloured, then remove from the pan and leave to drain on kitchen paper. Meanwhile in the other, fry the onion, pickles, capers, celery leaves and olives over a low heat for about 15 minutes. Add the sugar and wine vinegar and let the fumes of the wine vinegar evaporate for a minute or so, then stir in the aubergines and pine kernels. Heat through gently and serve warm, or leave to cool and serve cold.

Roast Potatoes with Onions, Garlic and Lemon
Patate Arrosto con Cipolle e Limone

One of the most delicious things about this potato dish is the flavour of the lemon juice, which seeps right through the potatoes and the garlic. When it comes to serving, usually the garlic cloves and the onions are eaten as well as the potatoes. The roasted garlic cloves can be just squeezed out of their skins by each person individually.

SERVES 4

4 medium-sized yellow-fleshed
   potatoes, scrubbed but not peeled

2 onions, thickly sliced

I head of garlic, separated
   but not peeled

I lemon, sliced

I tablespoon chopped
   fresh rosemary

6 tablespoons extra virgin olive oil

8 tablespoons water

I teaspoon dried oregano

Preheat the oven to 200°C/400°F/gas mark 6.

Cut the potatoes into fat, long chunks and place into a large, shallow roasting tin. Add the onions, unpeeled garlic cloves, lemon slices and rosemary. Toss well, add the oil, water and oregano and toss again. Bake in the oven for about 1 hour until tender, tossing a couple of times while cooking. Add a little extra water if the potatoes look like drying out.

Stuffed Peppers
Peperoni Imbottiti

These squashy, soft roasted peppers with their tangy stuffing make a great first course or accompaniment to a plain grilled fish or chicken dish. Green peppers are the traditional choice, but you could use other colours if you prefer.

SERVES 4

4 very large green peppers
   or 8 small ones

300 g (11 oz) stale bread,
   crusts removed

550 g (1¼ lb) canned
   tomatoes, seeded and
   chopped

1 tablespoon salted capers,
   rinsed and chopped

50g (2 oz) green olives, stoned and sliced

a fistful of fresh parsley, chopped

2 salted anchovies, boned, rinsed and chopped

75 g (3 oz) Pecorino cheese, freshly grated

150 ml (5 fl oz) olive oil

salt and freshly milled black pepper

Preheat the oven to 150°C/300°F/gas mark 3.

Wash and dry the peppers, then remove the stems and carefully scoop out the inside seeds and membranes. Soften the bread in a little water, then mix in about 4 tablespoons of the chopped tomatoes, the capers, olives, parsley, anchovies, Pecorino, about 3 tablespoons of the olive oil, the salt and pepper. Mix together very thoroughly, then spoon the mixture inside the peppers. Pour the remaining olive oil into an ovenproof dish and scatter the remaining tomatoes over it. Set the peppers upright in the dish and bake in the oven for 1 hour, basting frequently with the tomato and oil sauce which will form around them. Serve warm or cold.

Artichokes in Anchovy Sauce
Carciofi ai Succhi

Although this appears to be a totally bizarre recipe, it is as authentic as Etna herself and just as crazily Sicilian. I have always served this alongside cold fish dishes or as an antipasto, or as part of a buffet with lots of other cold dishes. Just for the record, a medium-sized artichoke is about the size of a man's clenched fist.

SERVES 8

12 medium-sized artichokes

6 onions, thinly sliced

6 tablespoons olive oil

8 tablespoons orange juice

8 tablespoons tangerine juice

4 tablespoons lemon juice

4 tablespoons white wine vinegar

1 teaspoon salt

3 tablespoons salted capers, rinsed

8 salted anchovies, boned and rinsed

1 teaspoon olive oil

2–3 tablespoons sugar

Remove the tough outer leaves from the artichokes, cut off the tops of the remaining leaves, then peel the stems and the bases. Cut each artichoke in half and remove the choke with the point of a sharp knife. Place the artichoke halves and the sliced onions in a large, heavy-based pan with the 6 tablespoons of olive oil, the juices, wine vinegar and salt. Add enough water barely to cover the artichokes, bring to a simmer, cover and cook very gently for 30–40 minutes until the artichokes are tender but still hold their shape.

Take the artichokes out of the pan and arrange them in a serving dish. Add the capers to the sauce and cook it gently, bubbling rhythmically until thickened and reduced. Place the anchovies and 1 teaspoon of olive oil in a bowl over a pan of simmering water and mix until dissolved. Add the melted anchovies and the sugar to the sauce and cook for a further 5 minutes or until the sugar is completely dissolved. Pour over the artichokes, leave to cool and serve cold.

Calabrese Potato and Onion Salad
Insalata Calabrese

This is the perfect potato salad for a barbecue as it has such a lot of tangy flavour to liven up and marry with the taste of chargrilled meat. I usually serve it with hamburgers flavoured with finely chopped red chilli and chopped black olives. And I realize it is not a Sicilian recipe, but one borrowed from Calabria, just seven kilometres across the Messina Straits!

SERVES 4

3 red onions, thinly sliced

4 fist-sized potatoes,
    scrubbed but not peeled

a pinch of salt

8 plum-shaped tomatoes,
    not over-ripe

5 fresh basil leaves, torn into shreds

I heaped teaspoon dried oregano

8 tablespoons olive oil

Soak the onions in cold water for 30 minutes. Cover the potatoes with cold salted water, bring to the boil, then boil until tender. Drain and leave aside until just cool enough to handle, then peel and slice thinly. Cut the tomatoes in half and remove the hard inner core. Slice the tomatoes and add them to the potatoes. Drain the onions carefully, dry them on kitchen paper, then add them to the potatoes and tomatoes. Add the basil, oregano, olive oil and a little salt. Toss everything together carefully and serve at once.

Courgettes in the Neapolitan Scapece Style
Zucchine a Scapece

This title is pronounced 'ska pay chay'. Although it is supposed to stand for a while before serving, it is unusual for anyone to be able to resist it for very long. If you don't have the equivalent of Sicilian sunshine to dry out the sliced courgettes, spread them on baking sheets and place in the oven at 140°C/275°F/ gas mark 1 for about an hour to dry out completely without colouring.

SERVES 4

6 large courgettes

olive oil for deep-frying

a handful of fresh mint,
  coarsely chopped

2 garlic cloves, finely chopped

4 tablespoons good-quality
  red or white wine vinegar

salt

Wash and dry the courgettes, top and tail them and then slice them lengthways. Place them on a wooden board, cover with a cloth and leave them in the sun to dry out for about 3 hours.

Heat about 10 cm (4 in) of olive oil in a large pan and fry all the courgettes until golden. Drain them carefully on kitchen paper, then transfer to a dish and sprinkle with mint, garlic, wine vinegar and salt. Cover and leave to stand for about 4 hours in a cool place, or overnight if possible.

Christmas Cauliflower Salad
Insalata di Rinforzo

Traditionally a Christmas recipe, the idea being that it sits on the side and various leftovers are added to it day by day to eke it out and make it last longer as the festivities unravel. If you want to follow that tradition, add potatoes, broccoli, tomatoes and other vegetables, which will blend well with the existing flavours. The dressing will need to be topped up accordingly. This salad is definitely more tasty if made the day before and allowed to rest overnight.

SERVES 4–6

I cauliflower, trimmed

salt

50 g (2 oz) black olives, stoned

50 g (2 oz) green olives, stoned

50 g (2 oz) pickled gherkins, chopped

50 g (2 oz) pickled red pepper, chopped

4 salted anchovies, boned, rinsed and cut
   into thin strips

6–9 tablespoons olive oil

½–2 tablespoons best-quality
   red wine vinegar

Boil the cauliflower whole in salted water until just tender, then cool and divide into florets. Place the cauliflower florets in a salad bowl and add the olives, gherkins and pickled red pepper. Mix together, then add the strips of anchovy and mix again. Dress with plenty of olive oil and a little wine vinegar. Add salt as necessary and leave the salad to chill for at least an hour before serving.

Plain Tomato Sauce
Il Sugo di Pomodoro

There are so many different versions of tomato sauce throughout the length and breadth of Italy, one could devote a small book to this subject alone. This is the most simple, fat-free and basic sauce, to which any number of other herbs or flavours can be added, and which changes completely in character depending on whether one adds butter or oil at the end. If the sauce comes out too liquid, just boil it fast until reduced. As well as using it for pasta, this sauce can be used as the basis for all sorts of savoury dishes from pizza or crostini toppings to soups.

SERVES 6

1 kg (2¼ lb) fresh tomatoes, peeled
  and quartered or canned tomatoes,
  drained and quartered

1 small onion, quartered

1 carrot, quartered

1 celery stick, quartered

1 large sprig of fresh parsley

7 fresh basil leaves

3 tablespoons olive oil

a pinch of salt

TO FINISH

1 tablespoon unsalted butter (optional)

OR 2 tablespoons extra virgin olive oil (optional)

Put all the ingredients except the salt into a pan. Cover and bring to the boil, then simmer for 30 minutes. Remove the lid and continue to simmer for about 20 minutes until most of the liquid has evaporated. Remove from the heat and push through a food mill or sieve. Season to taste with salt and reheat to serve.

If you want to enrich the flavour and texture, add either a tablespoon of unsalted butter or 2 tablespoons of extra virgin olive oil to the sauce as soon as it has been heated through. The ideas is not to cook the butter or oil but just to stir it through, so do this off the heat.

5 Desserts and Cakes

This is not just a collection of different possibilities for the sweet course to end your meal, but also of recipes for occasional treat-type dishes which can be served for afternoon tea, a mid-morning snack or any time you feel like it!

The dessert course is viewed very differently in Italy compared to some other countries because it is never assumed to be the most important part of the meal. Desserts tend to be as simple as a plate of hard almond biscuits to dunk into dessert wine or just a selection of fabulous fruit, and many families prefer to buy cakes or desserts from the *pasticceria* rather than making one themselves.

On the whole, Italy is not a nation of sweet-toothed people, although some of the oldest recipes are actually incredibly sweet, so there is something of a contradiction going on when it comes to the way Italians approach the question of pudding. Outside Italy, the world's most favourite and famed Italian pudding used to be Zabaglione (see page 170) but in recent years Tiramisu (see page 172) seems to have taken over from it, probably because it doesn't need 20 minutes of whisking time over a bain marie to get it right, but on the contrary it can be made a day ahead and chilled.

All this does not mean that Italy lacks dessert recipes, but simply that the interpretation of this course, or of sweet things in general, is different in Italy compared to the UK or the USA. After all, if all else fails, we have the world's most fantastic ice cream in literally hundreds of flavours to make up for what we might be perceived to lack in the pudding department!

Venetian Fritters
Frittelle Veneziane

This is the sort of thing you are likely to be served at parties in Venice, especially around Carnival time when the city erupts into festivities. They are particularly good when washed down with a glass or two of well-chilled Prosecco or a little Recioto di Soave, which is the region's best-loved dessert wine.

MAKES ABOUT 28

125 g (4½ oz) sultanas, soaked in tepid water for about 10 minutes, then drained and dried

2 tablespoons anisette or rum

500 g (1 lb 2 oz) plain white flour, sifted

75 g (3 oz) caster sugar

40 g (1½ oz) fresh yeast crumbled into 50 ml (2 fl oz) warm milk

extra warm milk for kneading

a pinch of salt

50 g (2 oz) pine kernels

50 g (2 oz) chopped candied peel

grated zest of 1 lemon

1 litre (1¾ pints) sunflower or olive oil

icing sugar, sifted

TO SERVE

chilled dessert wine or ice cream

Cover the sultanas with the anisette or rum and leave to soak until required.

Put the flour and sugar in a bowl. Make a hole in the centre and pour in the yeast and milk mixture. Mix together thoroughly, adding as much milk as required to make a smooth, soft dough. Mix in the salt, pine kernels, candied peel and lemon zest, then mix in the sultanas. Cover and leave to rise in a warm place for about 6 hours.

Knead the dough again, adding a little more milk if necessary to make the dough slightly wet so that you are able to spoon it. Heat the sunflower or olive oil in a deep pan until a small piece of bread dropped into the oil sizzles instantly. Fry tablespoonfuls of the fritter mixture in batches, dropping the batter carefully into the hot oil. As soon as the fritter returns to the surface, scoop it out of the pan and allow to drain on kitchen paper. Sprinkle with icing sugar and serve piping hot with chilled dessert wine or ice cream.

Ricotta Pudding
Budino di Ricotta

This dessert is delicious with warm poached fruits such as cherries, apricots, prunes, apples or pears. In winter time, poach the fruits with a handful of spices; in summer add a little lemon juice and zest. Sweeten the fruit to taste.

SERVES 4

400 g (14 oz) very fresh Ricotta cheese

50 g (2 oz) icing sugar, sifted

3 egg yolks

4 tablespoons dark rum

I tablespoon dessert wine

200 ml (7 fl oz) whipping cream, whipped until stiff

TO SERVE

sweet biscuits

Mix together the Ricotta, icing sugar and egg yolks until you have a thick, creamy texture. Stir in the rum and dessert wine, then fold in the whipped cream. Serve well chilled in stemmed glasses with sweet biscuits.

Polenta Cake
Torta di Polenta

This cake comes out like a very crumbly, thick biscuit. It is delicious with Zabaglione made with Prosecco (see page 170), or with lightly sweetened and whipped Mascarpone and raspberries or wild strawberries.

MAKES I X 20 CM (8 IN)
RATHER FLAT, CRISPY CAKE

300 g (11 oz) blanched almonds

300 g (11 oz) granulated sugar

300 g (11 oz) fine polenta flour

grated zest of I lemon

3 egg yolks

6 tablespoons single cream

a pinch of salt

Preheat the oven to 180C/350°F/gas mark 4.

Grind the almonds finely with the sugar. Mix with the polenta flour and the lemon zest. Mix in the egg yolks, cream and salt to make a loose but thick dough. Pour into a well-buttered 24 cm (9½ in) cake tin to a thickness of about 2 cm (¾ in) and bake for 20 minutes until firm and crisp, then turn on to a rack to cool.

Apple Charlotte
Charlotte di Mele

Serve this dessert with a little cold single cream or ice cream, or apple, vanilla or cinnamon ice cream, or a Zabaglione (see page 170) – which strictly speaking is a Piedmontese recipe when made with Prosecco rather than the usual Marsala. Prosecco is the Veneto's great sparkling white wine, very dry and refreshing with a fantastic flavour. The same dessert is delicious made with pears.

SERVES 8

FOR THE EGG CUSTARD

6 egg yolks

1 teaspoon plain
   white flour

4 tablespoons icing sugar

1½ teaspoons
   vanilla essence

1 litre (1¾ pints)
   full-cream milk

FOR THE FRUIT

1 kg (2¼ lb) apples such as Russet,
   which are good for both eating and cooking

500 g (1 lb 2 oz) sliced white bread,
   thinly buttered on each side

100 g (4 oz) granulated sugar

½ teaspoon ground cinnamon

3 tablespoons pine kernels

2 tablespoons chopped candied fruit

25 g (1 oz) unsalted butter

Preheat the oven to 180°C/350°F/gas mark 4.

First make the egg custard. Beat together the egg yolks, flour, icing sugar and vanilla essence in a heatproof bowl until pale yellow and thick. Heat the milk until just about to boil, then gradually beat it into the egg mixture. Place the bowl over a pan of steaming, simmering water and stir constantly for about 15–20 minutes until the custard coats the back of a spoon.

Peel and slice the apples. Grease an ovenproof dish large enough to take all the ingredients. Arrange a layer of buttered bread across the bottom, sprinkle the bread with sugar, then add a layer of apples, then a sprinkling each of cinnamon, pine kernels and candied fruit. Cover with the custard and repeat until all the ingredients have been used. Finish with a few dots of butter. Bake in the oven for about 30 minutes or until browned and set. Serve warm.

Veronese Pasta Cake
Torta di Paparele alla Veronese

This is one of my favourite cakes and whenever I make fresh pasta I always make a little bit extra so that I can use it to make a cake. It is really superb with the chocolate topping, especially if served warm, but it is also made without the chocolate in its native city of Verona.

MAKES I X 23 CM (9 IN) CAKE

350 g (12 oz) plain white flour

3 eggs

50 g (2 oz) unsalted butter, melted

a pinch of salt

200 g (7 oz) blanched almonds,
   finely chopped

200 g (7 oz) granulated sugar

grated zest of I lemon

6 tablespoons liqueur

2 tablespoons lemon juice

150 g (5 oz) good-quality
   plain chocolate, melted

Preheat the oven to 180°C/350°F/gas mark 4.

Measure 300 g (11 oz) of the flour on to a clean work surface. Make a hole in the centre, break the eggs into the hole and pour in the melted butter and the salt. Knead all this together to make a soft dough. Roll it out as thinly as possible and cut the dough into even ribbons with a sharp knife.

Butter a 23 cm (9 in) solid-based cake tin thoroughly and coat the inside with the remaining flour, shaking off any excess. In a bowl, mix together the almonds, sugar and lemon zest. Arrange a layer of pasta ribbons in the bottom of the cake tin, scatter with the almond mixture, sprinkle with the liqueur and cover with another layer of pasta ribbons. Continue until you have used all the ingredients, ending with pasta. Cover the top of the cake with a sheet of generously buttered baking parchment and bake in the oven for 55 minutes. Remove from the oven and sprinkle with the lemon juice. Run a knife around the edge of the cake and carefully remove it from the tin. Pour the melted chocolate all over the cake and allow to set slightly. Serve warm or cold. The cake should be moist and chewy.

Pumpkin Cake
Torta di Zucca

The quantities for this cake are calculated in raw weight of pumpkin, so in other words for a cake large enough for four you will need about 600 g (1 lb 5 oz) of pumpkin, double this for a larger cake. Choose your cake tin once you have made the batter. If you prefer, you can bake the pumpkin in the oven, then mash it with the butter once it is soft. The result is a very moist cake which is perfect with a scoop of rum and raisin ice cream.

SERVES 4

600 g (1 lb 5 oz) pumpkin, preferably
   the Barucca variety from Chioggia
150 g (5 oz) unsalted butter
a pinch of salt
150 g (5 oz) granulated sugar
50 g (2 oz) blanched almonds, crushed
50 g (2 oz) candied citron, chopped

50 g (2 oz) sultanas, soaked
   in a little grappa until swollen
grated zest of 1 lemon
75 g (3 oz) plain white flour
1 heaped teaspoon
   baking powder
2 eggs, separated
icing sugar, sifted

Preheat the oven to 180°C/350°C/gas mark 4.

Peel and cube the pumpkin, then put it into a pan with the butter and cook it for about 10 minutes until soft. Mash it thoroughly with the salt. Stir in the sugar, almonds, candied citron, the sultanas and grappa and the grated lemon zest. Beat all this together very thoroughly. Sift in the flour and the baking powder and stir. Beat the egg yolks until light and foamy, then fold in. Beat the egg whites until stiff, then fold in lightly. Turn into a greased and lined 20 cm (8 in) fairly shallow, solid-based cake tin and bake in the oven for about 1 hour or until a wooden skewer inserted in the centre of the cake comes out clean. Turn out on to a cooling rack, leave to cool, then dust with icing sugar to serve.

Bunet
Bunet

A marvellous combination of flavours here between the bittersweet of the amaretti biscuits, the chocolate and the coffee. You can turn this dessert out quite easily, in fact the first time I was served it, it had been baked in a loaf tin, which meant it could easily be sliced into neat sections. It is very rich, so needs nothing else to go with it, but if you do want to add something then it must be very cold single cream. If the flavour of amaretti biscuits is too strong, use Marie or morning coffee instead.

SERVES 6–8

1 litre (1¾ pints) milk

250 g (9 oz) amaretti biscuits

1 tablespoon drinking
    chocolate powder

6 eggs, beaten

150 g (5 oz) caster sugar

1–2 teaspoons instant coffee powder

6 tablespoons granulated sugar

2 tablespoons cold water

Preheat the oven to 160°C/325°F/gas mark 3.

Put the milk and amaretti biscuits in a pan, bring to the boil, then remove from the heat and break up the biscuits completely with a spoon. Stir in the chocolate powder. In a bowl, beat together the eggs and caster sugar thoroughly until pale and fluffy, then fold this mixture into the milk and amaretti mixture. Stir carefully to amalgamate perfectly, then stir in the coffee powder.

Put the granulated sugar and water into a small pan and heat very gently until the sugar has melted, brushing down any crystals from the sides of the pan. Continue to heat until the sugar has caramelized. Coat the bottom of six to eight moulds or ramekin dishes with the caramel. Divide the milk mixture evenly between the moulds and place them all in a roasting tin. Pour enough hot water around the moulds to come half way up their sides, then bake in the oven for 30 minutes or until a knife inserted into the centre of a mould comes out clean. Remove from the oven, cool and chill slightly before serving.

Marron and Chocolate Mountain
Il Montebianco

One of the most laborious jobs has always been the careful peeling of the marrons for this dessert, which in my home is served as the traditional alternative to Christmas pudding. Thankfully, there are now some ready-peeled and ready-puréed products available which are almost as fresh-tasting and delicious as freshly prepared marrons. This has the great advantage of making Montebianco a much more accessible dessert, which means it can be enjoyed as widely as it deserves to be. A potato ricer or food mill will be needed for this dish.

SERVES 10

1 kg (2¼ lb) fresh, plump chestnuts, marrons if possible

OR 750 g (1½ lb) ready-peeled chestnuts or ready-made chestnut purée

300 g (11 oz) granulated or caster sugar

124 ml (4½ fl oz) cold water

a pinch of salt

4 tablespoons strega liqueur (optional)

750 ml (1¼ pints) double or whipping cream, whipped

1½ tablespoons icing sugar, sifted

1 teaspoon vanilla essence

6 large meringues, crumbled

150 g (5 oz) good-quality plain chocolate with at least 60% cocoa solids

2 tablespoons best-quality drinking chocolate

TO DECORATE

6 marrons glacés

12 candied violets

½ vanilla pod

If you are using fresh chestnuts, preheat the oven to 200°C/400°F/gas mark 6. Cut a cross in each chestnut, lay them on a baking sheet and bake for 15 minutes or until the skins begin to curl around where they have been cut. Take them out of the oven and peel them while they are still hot, then set them aside.

Put the sugar and water in a pan and heat gently until the syrup reaches 102°C/215°F when the syrup forms a fine thread when a drop is dipped into cold water and pulled between the back of two spoons. Add the cooked and peeled or ready-peeled chestnuts to the syrup with the salt and poach very gently for about 30 minutes. Drain the chestnuts, put into a separate bowl, then pour over the liqueur. Whether you have boiled the chestnuts or are using purée, boil the syrup over a medium heat until reduced by one-third. Drain the liqueur from the chestnuts, discard any excess liquid and pour over the syrup. If using chestnut purée, mix the purée, reduced syrup and liqueur together thoroughly.

Whip the cream, icing sugar and vanilla essence until it holds a peak, then divide into three bowls. Mix three of the crushed meringues into one bowl. Halve the chocolate and chop one half finely. Mix this into the second bowl of cream. Leave the other bowl of cream plain. Chill the cream until required.

Shave the remaining chocolate into long curls, or melt in a heatproof bowl set over a pan of hot water until runny. Push the marrons through a ricer or food mill, or push through a colander, so that they fall in strands on to a serving platter, making a mound shape. Cover with the first layer of chocolate cream, then a layer of meringue cream, then finally most of the plain cream. None of these layers needs to be smooth and even, they can all overlap and be as uneven as you like. Crumble the remaining meringue on top of the mound to symbolize the white peak, and spoon plain white cream around the peak. Decorate the slopes with chocolate shavings or melted chocolate and a fine dusting of drinking chocolate around the base. Chill and serve within 6–8 hours. Just before serving, arrange the marrons glacés and candied violets around the base for decoration.

Zabaglione
Zabaglione

Here is the most classic of all Italian desserts. It is not as easy as it looks and it will separate very quickly if you haven't cooked it enough.

SERVES 6

6 egg yolks

4 tablespoons cold water

6 tablespoons Prosecco or Marsala

6 tablespoons caster sugar

Put all the ingredients into the top of a double boiler or in a heatproof bowl set over a pan of barely simmering water. Whisk constantly with a balloon whisk or hand-held electric whisk, keeping an even rhythm and always beating in the same direction. Whisk for about 20 minutes until the mixture has become light, foamy and pale yellow and the consistency of semi-melted ice cream. If the mixture appears to be scrambling, remove from the heat and beat hard until smooth. Never allow the water to boil. Serve warm or cold in stemmed glasses.

Panna Cotta
Panna Cotta

This delicious Piedmontese speciality is gaining popularity and fame all over Italy and beyond. You can make it completely plain or add crushed amaretti biscuits, coffee, chocolate, soft fruits, lemon or orange zest, a dash of liqueur – the possibilities are endless. The skill of the dessert lies in getting it to set without being at all rubbery, so just the right amount of sheet gelatine needs to be used. Recently, I made 200 of these for a party and once they had set, discovered I had been over-generous on the gelatine so I had to throw them away and start all over again!

SERVES 8

1 litre (1¾ pints) single cream

8 tablespoons icing sugar, sifted

3–4 sheets of gelatine

FOR THE FLAVOURING

grated rind of 1 lemon

OR 1 small cup of espresso coffee

OR **3 tablespoons liqueur or brandy**

OR **2 teaspoons vanilla essence**

FOR THE CARAMEL

4 tablespoons caster sugar

TO DECORATE

a sprinkling of coffee, a grating of lemon rind

or a fruit coulis to match the chosen flavouring

Divide the cream equally between two separate pans and bring to just under the boil. Add the icing sugar to one pan and add the gelatine to the other. Whisk both halves constantly until the sugar and gelatine have completely dissolved and the cream is very hot but not boiling. Pour both halves into one bowl and whisk together. Add the flavouring of your choice and stir. Leave to cool completely, stirring occasionally.

While the mixture is cooling, coat the bottom of eight small flameproof moulds with caster sugar and melt the sugar over a low heat to caramelize. Alternatively, place the sugar in a small pan and heat gently until golden, then pour it into the moulds. Allow to cool.

Strain the panna cotta into the caramelized moulds and place in the fridge to set until required. Decorate with a sprinkling of coffee, a grating of lemon rind, a fruit coulis or whatever is appropriate to your chosen flavour.

Tiramisu
Tiramisù

Currently the most fashionable of all Italian desserts, you can make Tiramisu in individual stemmed glasses if you prefer. You can use almost any liqueur. I don't recommend sambuca, but amaretto is delicious. It is best if made a day in advance. Please note that this recipe does contain raw eggs.

SERVES 6

250 g (9 oz) Mascarpone or very rich cream cheese

4 eggs, separated

4 tablespoons caster sugar

2 teaspoons espresso coffee

100 g (4 oz) bitter cooking chocolate, broken into small pieces

8 tablespoons weak coffee

6 tablespoons rum, brandy, Tia Maria or other liqueur

about 20 savoiardi or boudoir biscuits

2 teaspoons cocoa

2 teaspoons instant coffee powder

Whisk the cheese until soft and manageable. Beat the egg yolks until pale, then whisk them into the cheese. Gradually add the sugar, stirring and whisking constantly. Pour in the espresso coffee and mix thoroughly. Beat the egg whites until very stiff, then fold them into the mixture. Gently stir in the chocolate.

Mix together the weak coffee and liqueur. Dip half the biscuits in this mixture one at a time, then use them to line the bottom of a bowl. Spoon in half the cheese mixture. Dip the remaining biscuits in the liquid and arrange them over the cheese. Pour over the remaining cheese mixture. Bang the dish down lightly to settle the layers. Mix the cocoa and coffee powder and sift over the dessert. Chill for at least 3 hours, preferably overnight.

Almond Dunking Biscuits
Biscottini di Prato

Although these biscuits will never be quite the same as the commercially made variety, they still taste delicious. Italians love to dunk, and these biscuits are made to be dunked into a glass of Vinsanto, Tuscany's best-loved sweet dessert wine, for a very simple dessert.

SERVES 6

250 g (9 oz) blanched
  almonds

1 kg (2¼ lb) plain white flour

8 eggs, beaten

1 kg (2¼ lb) caster sugar

½ teaspoon bicarbonate of soda

a pinch of salt

Preheat the oven to 150°C/300°F/gas mark 2.

Lay the almonds on a baking sheet and toast them under the grill for about 5 minutes until golden, then chop them coarsely.

Tip the flour on to a work top and make a hollow in the centre. Pour the eggs, sugar, bicarbonate of soda and salt into the hollow and knead into a dough, then add the almonds. Knead everything together very thoroughly, then shape it with your hands into several 10 cm (4 in) long, thick strips about 6 cm (2½ in) wide and 3 cm (1¼ in) thick. Slide the strips of dough on to oiled baking sheets and bake in the oven for about 7 minutes until just golden. Take them out of the oven and cut the strips into 2 cm (¾ in) wide biscuits on the diagonal. Return to the oven for a further 6 minutes until they are very crunchy and crisp. They will keep for several months in an airtight container.

Fruit Tart with Vanilla and Lemon Mascarpone

Crostata di Frutta con Mascarpone alla Vaniglia e Limone

In Tuscany, this would be served on its own without cream but you might prefer to serve it warm with a little single or double cream or with this vanilla and lemon Mascarpone.

MAKES I X 25 CM (10 IN) TART

300 g (11 oz) plain white flour

150 g (5 oz) caster sugar

a pinch of salt

grated zest of 1 lemon

2 eggs

150 g (5 oz) unsalted butter, softened

300 g (11 oz) fruit of your choice
  such as plums, cherries, peaches
  or apricots, stoned

a pinch of ground cinnamon

1 egg yolk, beaten

FOR THE VANILLA AND LEMON MASCARPONE

250 g (9 oz) Mascarpone cheese

100 ml (3¼ fl oz) double cream

juice of 1 lemon

1 vanilla pod, seeds only

50 g (2 oz) icing sugar, sifted

2 tablespoons Marsala or Vinsanto

Mix together the flour, 50 g (2 oz) of the sugar, the salt and lemon zest. Pile the mixture on to a work top and make a hollow in the centre with your fist. Break the eggs into the hollow and add the butter. Knead together quickly to form a smooth ball of pastry. Wrap it in a cloth and put it in a cool place (not the fridge) to rest for about 20 minutes. Meanwhile, stew the fruit gently with the remaining sugar and the cinnamon until it forms a sort of thick jam. Leave to cool.

To make the vanilla and lemon Mascarpone, cream all the ingredients together carefully and chill for 1 hour.

Preheat the oven to 190°C/375°F/gas mark 5.

Divide the dough into two sections, one slightly larger than the other. Roll out the larger piece and use to line a greased and lightly floured 25 cm (10 in) flan ring. Fill with the cooled fruit. Roll out the smaller piece of pastry and cut into strips. Arrange the strips as a lattice over the fruit. Brush lightly with the egg yolk and bake in the oven for about 20 minutes until golden brown. Leave to cool before serving on its own or with the Mascarpone cream.

Sweet Grape Pizza
Schiacciata d'Uva

This kind of sweet bread is made around the time of the wine harvest when there are plenty of grapes around. You need to squash the grapes down and into the focaccia base, using plenty of sugar on top to bring out the flavour of the fruit. The end result looks absolutely beautiful and tastes delicious, especially when served for breakfast.

MAKES 6

FOR THE PIZZA DOUGH

550 g (1¼ lb) strong plain
   white flour

2 sachets of easy-blend
   dried yeast

½ teaspoon salt

½ teaspoon caster sugar

3 tablespoons olive oil

350 ml (12 fl oz) warm water

500 g (1 lb 2 oz) fresh black or
   white grapes, hulled

12 tablespoons granulated sugar

To make the dough, mix the flour, yeast, salt and sugar in a food processor. Add the oil and gradually add enough of the water to make a dough. Process until smooth and elastic. Place in an oiled bowl, cover with clingfilm and leave in a warm place for 1 hour until doubled in size.

Preheat the oven to 220°C/425°F/gas mark 7.

Divide the dough into six equal sections. Roll each one out to a circle and place them on well-oiled baking sheets. Sprinkle the surface of each one with a little oil, then cover with grapes, pressing them down into the dough. Sprinkle with the sugar and bake in the oven for 15–20 minutes or until the dough and the grapes are cooked through. Serve warm or cold.

Panforte
Panforte

A rich and sweet Italian classic, this needs to be served in very thin slices either as a dessert or with coffee. You can dust the finished panforte with sifted icing sugar for an overall white finish if you wish.

MAKES 750 G (1¾ LB)

200 g (7 oz) unblanched almonds

250 g (9 oz) chopped candied peel

125 g (4½ oz) shelled walnuts

50 g (2 oz) candied orange peel, chopped

200 g (7 oz) plain white flour

1 teaspoon ground cinnamon

½ teaspoon ground allspice

½ teaspoon ground coriander

350 g (12 oz) caster sugar

1 heaped tablespoon clear honey

sheets of edible paper

FOR DUSTING

1 tablespoon ground cinnamon

1 tablespoon icing sugar

Preheat the oven to 150°C/300°F/gas mark 2.

Blanch and peel 150 g (5 oz) of the almonds by soaking them in hot water for about 1 minute, then removing the skins. Toast the blanched almonds in the oven or under the grill until golden, then chop them finely. Put in a food processor with the chopped candied peel, walnuts and orange peel and process until well blended. Take out of the bowl and place on a work surface. Combine with the remaining unblanched almonds, the flour and spices.

Melt the sugar and honey together and heat to 120°C/248°F when the syrup will thicken and begin to turn dark golden. Remove from the heat immediately, pour over the dry ingredients and mix well with a spatula, then with your hands when the mixture has cooled a little. Make sure you do not touch the hot syrup. When everything is well amalgamated, press the mixture into a 25 cm (10 in) tin, base-lined with edible paper, and level the top. Sift together the cinnamon and icing sugar and dust over the top of the panforte. Bake in the oven for 30 minutes. Leave to cool before removing from the tin, then serve cut into very thin slices. Store in an airtight container.

Nut and Chocolate Dessert
Zuccotto

This delicious pudding is meant to look like the traditional helmet of a Tuscan mercenary going into battle, which in turn was named after a small, rounded pumpkin! The most difficult bit is doing the stencilling. If you prefer, just dust with icing sugar, then lightly dust with cocoa powder on top. This is a great dessert to keep as a standby in the freezer. You can make two smaller bowls if you wish.

SERVES 8

75 g (3 oz) shelled hazelnuts

1 x 25 cm (10 in) basic
  sponge cake

6 tablespoons brandy

4 tablespoons amaretto
  or other sweet liqueur

1 litre (1¾ pints) whipping cream

75 g (3 oz) blanched almonds, coarsely chopped

2 tablespoons plain chocolate drops or chips

2 tablespoons chopped mixed candied peel
  or glacé fruits

150 g (5 oz) icing sugar, sifted

100 g (4 oz) good-quality plain chocolate,
  melted and cooled

2 tablespoons cocoa powder

Toast the hazelnuts on a baking sheet under the grill until dark brown, then rub off the skin and chop the nuts. Cut off the top crust and sides of the cake and use for another dish. Slice the cake in half horizontally, then slice into strips. Line a large, round bowl with foil. Press the strips of cake against the sides of the bowl, using the brandy and liqueur to make them stick. Set aside.

In a second bowl, whip the cream until stiff, then fold in the hazelnuts, almonds, chocolate drops, candied peel and 100 g (4 oz) of the sugar, folding it in carefully. Line the bottom and sides of the cake-lined bowl with half the cream, and make a hollow in the centre. Stir the melted chocolate into the remaining cream and use the chocolate cream to fill the hollow in the centre. Level the top with a spatula. Place the bowl in the fridge for at least 3 hours.

Meanwhile, draw a circle slightly larger than the bowl on a sheet of stiff paper, then draw diameter lines to divide the circle into eight. Number the wedges 1 to 8 and cut out the wedge numbers 2, 4, 6 and 8, leaving the paper joined at the centre.

Turn the dessert out on to a flat platter. Remove the foil and dust with the remaining icing sugar. Hold the cut paper on the top and dust the cake again with the cocoa powder. Remove the paper. You should have alternate segments of brown and white on the surface. Freeze for 2 hours, then chill until required.

Rice Cake
Torta di Riso

It is the rich, eggy quality of this cake which makes it so delicious. We used to be given this for tea when we were children as there was an idea that all the eggs and milk were really nourishing and good for us. When I make it these days, I sometimes add chopped candied fruits, sultanas or nuts to the basic mixture, just to make it a bit more interesting. Do not use a loose-bottomed tin to make this cake, or all the liquid will ooze away.

MAKES 1 x 25 CM (10 IN) CAKE

150 g (5 oz) short-grain rice

1.2 litres (2 pints) milk

25 g (1 oz) unsalted butter

2 tablespoons semolina

8 eggs

250 g (9 oz) caster sugar

3 tablespoons brandy

juice of ½ lemon

OR grated zest of ½ lemon

Preheat the oven to 180°C/350°F/gas mark 4.

Put the rice and about two-thirds of the milk into a pan, bring to the boil, then boil for 10 minutes. Drain. Generously butter a 25 cm (10 in) solid-based, deep cake tin, then sprinkle with the semolina, turning the tin upside-down to shake out any loose semolina.

Beat the eggs in a large bowl until foaming and pale yellow. Gradually add the sugar, beating constantly, then add the brandy and lemon juice or zest. Stir thoroughly, then add the rice and all the remaining milk. Pour into the cake tin and bake in the oven for about 50 minutes until a wooden skewer inserted in the centre comes out clean. The cake should be well set and golden brown. Serve warm or cold.

Garfagnana Almond Cake
Torta Garfagnina

This simple cake is often served as a teatime treat in my area of Tuscany, although in some households it also graces the table at breakfast time. It is traditionally very plain, so you might like to split it and fill it with a good-quality apricot or peach jam if you want to liven it up a bit.

MAKES I x 30 CM (12 IN) CAKE

75 g (3 oz) blanched almonds

½ teaspoon almond essence

175 g (6 oz) unsalted butter

500 g (1 lb 2 oz) plain white flour

200 g (7 oz) granulated sugar

1 teaspoon fennel seeds

grated zest of 1 lemon

3 eggs, beaten

50 ml (2 fl oz) sweet liqueur of your choice, such as amaretto, sambuca, strega or genepy

1 teaspoon cream of tartar

1 teaspoon bicarbonate of soda

150 ml (5 fl oz) milk, warm

Preheat the oven to 160°C/325°F/gas mark 3.

Grind the almonds very finely, then mix them with the almond essence. Use some of the butter to grease a 30 cm (12 in) cake tin very thoroughly, then dust the tin with a little of the flour, shaking off any excess. Melt the remaining butter, then leave it to cool. Sift the remaining flour into a large mixing bowl. Stir in the sugar, ground almonds, fennel seeds and lemon zest. Mix in the eggs, melted butter and liqueur. Beat the mixture thoroughly. Stir the cream of tartar and the bicarbonate of soda into the milk. Pour this into the cake mixture and beat again. Pour the cake mixture into the prepared tin and bake in the oven for about 1 hour or until a wooden skewer inserted into the centre of the cake comes out perfectly dry and clean. Serve warm or cold.

Almond Kisses
Bocconetti di Mandorla

These are delicious with coffee, although when they go wrong, they can go spectacularly flat! The oven temperature is crucial. *Zuccata* is candied pumpkin and is widely used in Sicilian confectionery and patisserie but you can use any other candied or crystallized fruit.

MAKES 36

450 g (1 lb) blanched almonds

200 g (7 oz) caster sugar

½ teaspoon vanilla essence

3 egg whites

about 6 tablespoons *zuccata*

Preheat the oven to 150°C/300°F/gas mark 2.

Grind the almonds to a fairly fine meal. Stir in the sugar, then the vanilla essence. Beat the egg whites until they form soft peaks, then fold them into the almonds. Mix to a workable paste. Shape a tablespoon of the mixture into a ball, poke a hole in it, and fill the hole with ½ teaspoon of *zuccata*. Cover the hole with a little more of the almond mixture and roll gently until it is a well-sealed ball little more than 2.5 cm (1 in) in diameter. Repeat with the rest of the mixture. Place the balls on greased and floured baking sheets and bake in the oven for about 25 minutes or until delicately browned.

Almond Milk
Latte di Mandorle

Ideally, include ten per cent bitter almonds (*mandorle amare*) in the almond mixture for this cooling drink, which is served on the hottest Sicilian days. If bitter almonds prove hard to find, substitute dried-out kernels from peach stones.

SERVES 2

500 g (1 lb 2 oz) freshest possible ground blanched almonds

5–6 tablespoons sugar

about 500 ml (17 fl oz) cold water

Mix the almonds with the sugar and place in a muslin bag. Soak the bag in the water for about 1 hour. Dip the bag in the water, then wring it out until the liquid looks milky white and there is no more milk coming out of the almonds. Chill well.

Cinnamon Jelly
Gelo di Cannella

If you prefer a clearer jelly, you can use sheet or powdered gelatine instead of the cornflour. In this case, you will add two sheets of gelatine to the liquid once you have strained it and returned it to the boil. The flavour of cinnamon is incredibly intense and surprisingly refreshing. This is a very light and absolutely delicious dessert which looks very pretty when set on top of a vine leaf and decorated with a few edible flowers.

SERVES 6

10 g (⅓ oz) cinnamon sticks

800 ml (1⅓ pints) cold water

300 g (11 oz) caster sugar

65 g (2¼ oz) cornflour

50 g (2 oz) good-quality plain chocolate, broken into pieces

a few lemon leaves to decorate

Put the cinnamon sticks and cold water into a pan. Place over a medium heat and bring to the boil, then boil gently for about 5 minutes. Remove from the heat and leave to stand for 12 hours.

Strain the cinnamon liquid carefully, return to the pan and add the sugar. Dissolve the cornflour in 2 tablespoons of the cinnamon liquid, then add to the rest of the ingredients in the pan. Bring to the boil, stirring constantly, then boil very gently until thickened, stirring constantly. Remove from the heat and add the chocolate. Stir until the chocolate has melted. Turn into one large or six small, individual moulds and chill until solid. Turn out and serve decorated with a few lemon leaves.

Lemon Granita
Granita di Limone

This is like a simple lemon sorbet. It is very refreshing and can help you to feel a lot less full after a heavy meal. In Italy, it would be eaten either as a light dessert or just to help you cool off. It is also delicious with a mixed citrus fruit salad.

SERVES 8–10

200 g (7 oz) granulated sugar

1.6 litres (2¾ pints) cold water

250 ml (8 fl oz) freshly squeezed lemon juice

To make a syrup, place the sugar in 400 ml (14 fl oz) of the water in a pan, bring to the boil, then boil long enough to dissolve all the sugar. Allow to cool, then add the remaining water and the lemon juice. Stir well and pour into a shallow aluminium pan (a cake tin is perfect). Place in the freezer for 30 minutes.

Remove from the freezer and scrape down the sides and bottom of the pan, breaking up the part that has solidified and blending it into that which is still liquid. Repeat this process every 30 minutes until the granita has become a fairly firm, flaky slush. Remove the granita from the pan and ideally serve it at once. If you are not eating it immediately, transfer it to a sealable glass or plastic container. If you leave it too long in the metal container it will 'burn' – that is the water will separate and form ice crystals.

Sicilian Cassata
La Cassata Siciliana

This amazingly rich and sumptuous Sicilian classic is traditionally made in the spring. It has its origins buried deep in Sicily's culinary history, taking its name from the Arab word meaning 'big round bowl'. It used to be made by the nuns of Palermo's convents, who would sell the cassata to members of the parish. At one stage they became so absorbed in making cassata that they began to neglect their prayers and holy duties and consequently received a severe reprimand from their archbishop.

SERVES 4

500 g (1 lb 2 oz) very fresh
   Ricotta cheese

300 g (11 oz) icing sugar, sifted

1 teaspoon vanilla essence

3 tablespoons rum or liqueur

3 tablespoons splintered
   good-quality plain chocolate

3 tablespoons chopped mixed candied peel

300 g (11 oz) basic sponge cake, cut in thin slices

6 tablespoons basic egg custard (see page 163)

TO DECORATE

pale green fondant icing

flakes of chocolate, candied and glacé fruit,
   silver and coloured dragees, sugared almonds,
   rice paper flowers

Push the Ricotta through a sieve, then blend it lightly with the icing sugar until it is of the consistency of lightly whipped cream. Flavour it with the vanilla essence and rum or liqueur. Mix in the chocolate splinters and candied peel. Line a 15 cm (6 in) bowl or pudding basin with foil or baking parchment, then line it with slices of sponge cake, using the custard to cement the slices together securely. Fill with the Ricotta mixture, levelling the top carefully. Put a plate on the top and press it down, then place it in the fridge for about 2–3 hours.

Turn the cassata out on to a plate and ice it carefully with the soft fondant icing. Decorate as much as possible with chocolate flakes, candied fruit, coloured dragees or whatever else you choose. Chill until required.

Ricotta Fritters
Cassateddi di Ricotta

These fritters are a bit messy and fiddly to make, but they taste delicious if the Ricotta is really fresh and sweet. Make sure you roll out the dough really fine, otherwise you'll end up with a lot of filling left over.

MAKES 36

FOR THE DOUGH

500 g (1 lb 2 oz) plain
   white flour

3 tablespoons caster sugar

2 tablespoons cocoa powder

250 ml (8 fl oz) dry white wine

90 g (3½ oz) lard, butter or
   margarine, diced

FOR THE FILLING

750 g (1¾ lb) Ricotta cheese, well drained

200 g (7 oz) granulated sugar

75 g (3 oz) good-quality plain chocolate, grated

OR grated rind of 1 lemon

TO FINISH

vegetable oil for frying

5 tablespoons icing sugar, sifted

1 teaspoon ground cinnamon

Sift together the flour, sugar and cocoa on to a marble or wooden surface. Make a well in the centre and gradually add the wine, using as much as it takes to make a fairly solid, thick dough. Gradually knead the lard, butter or margarine, piece by piece, into the dough. Knead for about 15 minutes, rolling the dough out into a long strip, then folding it back on to itself and rolling it out again. Incorporate as much air into the dough as possible, working it until it is shiny and elastic, but not greasy. Put the dough into a bowl, cover with a cloth or a lid and let it rest for at least 1 hour.

Meanwhile, make the filling. Sieve the Ricotta, then mix it thoroughly with the sugar, beating vigorously. Mix in the chocolate or lemon rind.

Roll out the dough to a very thin sheet and cut out into 7.5 cm (3 in) disks. On each disk, place a scant tablespoonful of the Ricotta mixture. Fold the disks over into half moons and, moistening the edges with water, seal them securely.

Heat a pan of vegetable oil at least 10 cm (4 in) deep. Fry the fritters in the piping hot oil, in batches if necessary, for a few minutes until golden brown and crisp. Drain on kitchen paper and serve warm, sprinkled with icing sugar and ground cinnamon.

Baked Peaches with Amaretti and Marsala
Pesche Ripiene al Forno con Amaretti e Marsala

This delicious way of serving peaches is especially good when made with the end-of-season peaches that tend to be a bit on the woolly side. You can also make the same dish with apricots, large plums or nectarines. Try serving it warm with a scoop of vanilla or almond ice cream.

SERVES 6

6 large peaches of the
   variety which will
   split in half quite easily
6 amaretti biscuits, finely
   crumbled

50 g (2 oz) good-quality
   plain chocolate, grated
50 g (2 oz) granulated sugar
25 g (1 oz) blanched almonds, chopped
150 ml (5 fl oz) sweet Marsala

Preheat the oven to 190°C/375°F/gas mark 5.

Wash the peaches and cut them in half. Remove the stones and scoop out about half of the flesh, leaving a layer of flesh over the skins. Mash the removed flesh with the crumbled amaretti, grated chocolate, sugar and almonds. Dampen this mixture with a little Marsala, just enough to make a sticky texture. Fill all the peaches evenly with the mixture. Arrange the peaches in an ovenproof dish and surround with the rest of the Marsala. Cover loosely with foil and bake in the oven for about 30 minutes until the peaches are tender, basting occasionally with the wine. Remove the foil and increase the oven temperature for a few minutes to make the tops of the peaches slightly crisp, or slide under the grill for about 5 minutes. Serve hot or cold.

Index